RICHARD DIMBLEBY, BROADCASTER

This change in the Dimbleby fortunes put an end to Richard's hopes of going on from his public school to Oxford or Edinburgh and eventually becoming a surgeon. Instead he put on an apron and was set to work at F. W. Dimbleby and Sons Ltd to learn all about printing and the newspaper business. He was taught to set type and to write copy. He covered police court cases and organised advertising.

His mother, née Gwendoline Bolwell, had a pleasant contralto voice. She used to sing to young Richard and his sister Patricia. She also used to sing for the Richmond Operatic Society, in musicals such as 'Rose Marie',

Aged 10, with mother Gwen and sister Pat

'The Desert Song' and 'The Vagabond King'. Indeed the Dimbleby background held elements of show business as well as journalism. Richard's father was on the business-management side of the Richmond Operatic Society, and Richard himself loved the weeks when at the age of twelve he acted as call boy. At Mill Hill he played Ralph Rackstraw in the school production of Gilbert and Sullivan's 'H.M.S. Pinafore', and throughout his broadcasting career he relished being produced as an actor enjoys good direction.

Richard Dimbleby was also a talented pianist and organist. Later, on countless occasions in all parts of the world he was to entertain friends with improvisations at the piano. He was the first to play publicly on the new organ at the Festival Hall, and once the London air rang out with 'Oranges and Lemons' when Richard played the bells at All Hallows Church at the Tower. Music and messing about in boats were always his main sources of relaxation.

By twenty-three he had had a thorough grounding in journalism, and plenty of energy, enthusiasm and self-confidence. But he had no experience at all of broadcasting.

L. F. Lewis, now the Engineer in charge of Sound Outside Broadcasts, was told to take the BBC's only mobile recording van to the model engineering exhibition at the Royal Horticultural Hall in London, and look out for a rosy-faced young man outside the entrance. 'For goodness sake help me,' Richard said. 'This is my very first BBC job.' Twenty-four hours later he told Lewis, 'It's all right, I'm in.' He was, but only just.

B

5

Tony Wigan, BBC United Nations Correspondent, was then chief sub-editor. He recalls:

'H.M.S. Pinafore' at
Mill Hill School, 1928

'He very nearly didn't make it. His very first broadcast in the nine-thirty News was heard by the Director-General, then Sir John Reith, to us both a deeply respected and rather frightening man. The Newsroom phone rang three times, the signal that the D.G. was on the line. He enquired the name of the reporter in the News and on being told said only that he never wanted to hear him again. But Dimbleby was given another chance and matters arranged themselves.'

Arthur Phillips, a Programme Assistant with the mobile recording van, went with him on his first actuality news broadcast which came from a cow-shed near Amesbury, hardly an auspicious beginning for a great broadcasting career.

'Cherry, a champion cow, had broken the milking record and Richard Dimbleby was sent down to cover this great event. We went down together with the recording van and by the light of a hurricane lamp – and with Cherry breathing steamily over his shoulder – Richard made his first radio interview. He put up the microphone and said "Moo" – and she mooed. But this was only half the job; the recordings which were required for the ten o'clock News had to be edited and transmitted from the Bournemouth studio, a very primitive lash-up of a place over a cycle shop. Just before transmission the only gramophone turntable in the place completely gave up the ghost and nothing would make it rotate.

'Writing of this some years later, Richard said, "As the ten o'clock News approached I was in despair. To tell the truth, I had an unpleasant feeling that if my first effort at broadcasting was a failure I might lose my nerve and never be able to do the job at all." But his anxiety was never apparent to me as I turned the record with my finger for the duration of the broadcast. As he said later, "The whole thing went off like a dream, and no one in the world was happier than I, though the memory of it made me tremble."

6

'He tackled his news reporting with zest and tireless enthusiasm; floods in the fens, gales on the Welsh coast, an interview with William Morris, the motor magnate, a shipwreck, a stranded Cornish lighthouse keeper, were some of his early assignments, and recording engineers L. F. Lewis, Harvey Sarney and myself spent many hours in his ancient Morris Oxford being driven at breakneck speed about the countryside. We were always reluctant to sit in the front seat with Richard, for when it got dark and the engine warmed up you could see the exhaust manifold glowing white hot through a hole in the floorboards, and when you complained the answer you got was – "Nothing to be afraid of, it's done thousands of miles like that". It had, too.

'Dimbleby was not yet a household word. There were inevitably times when it was either mispronounced or misspelled. Before the war he was to report on some fleet exercises off Gibraltar, and in the harbour a destroyer steamed alongside the P & O liner that had taken him out from England and a voice called over the loud hailer, "Have you a Mr Soapleby aboard?" He was Mr Soapleby for the rest of the exercise, preferring the Ward Room's mild amusement at this rather odd name to the mirth he thought there would have been had he told them of their mistake.'

Ralph Murray, now the British Ambassador in Athens, was then in charge of the News Talks Section and was Dimbleby's first mentor in the BBC.

SIR RALPH MURRAY

Dogsbody in the Newsroom

Richard was, or seemed, a mere boy when he joined us in 1936. He was twenty-three. We were all pretty young, and he was five years younger than us all. We were blundering about among the problems and experiments of expanding the News Service. It had been a very modest affair of sub-edited agency news. Our ideas of expansion involved re-negotiation of contracts with the agencies to give us greater freedom of action, expansion of bulletins both in length and frequency, and the introduction into them of our own reports or illustrations or contributions on outstanding events both at home and abroad. Kenneth Adam's restless spirit, untamed by two years on the *Manchester Guardian*, was stirring this pot; Tony Wigan had come from Belfast to apply his severe sub-editing standards; Angus Mackay from Edinburgh was licking the sports news into shape; Charles Gardner was a sub-editor then, too; others played their parts. I was in charge, on a shoe-string budget, of the beginnings of the reporting expansion, and to me Richard Dimbleby was assigned.

He was allotted of course the role of stooge, junior reporter, dogsbody, help. We were experimenting with our techniques, for which there was no precedent. We were not only young, we were mostly a graduate lot with some serious thoughts and criteria between us, most of us had more or less newspaper or news agency experience, a fair aggregate of intelligence and large areas of ignorance. We thought however we knew most of the answers. Richard was not only five years younger than the bulk of us – the exception was our dear, infuriating, experienced, scholarly, unreasonable and highly skilled old Scots news editor, the late R. T. Clark – he was not a graduate.

Richard brought to our team a tradition of newspaper ownership and management, which he had learned in his family newspapers, and a personal enthusiasm for reporting – but *not* the severe training of sub-editing. Mentally, he was the antithesis of all of us, whether of the slightly conceited, sceptical young graduates or of the disciplined, self-critical professional sub-editors. He was enthusiastic, uncritical, unintellectual. He not only knew none of the answers, he never even bothered about the questions. We nicknamed him, affectionately and artlessly, Bumble, because he was fat and buzzed: he was never either clumsy or pompous. But he had charm and immense self-confidence.

Now self-confidence in a journalist is vital. His profession constantly requires him to describe, judge, criticise or examine matters on which he necessarily cannot possibly possess much if any expertise, and in relation to which not only his judgment but even his description must rest on incomplete information. He must have the confidence, perhaps one should say the *blind* confidence, constantly to pronounce his judgment or publish his findings on this inadequate foundation, or he will break his heart and certainly will be a bad journalist. Plenty have it, and become in various degrees perspicacious, opinionated, analytical, waspish or portentous as their natures and professional opportunities

With Arthur Phillips (left)
and Charles Gardner
editing news recordings

8

allow. Perhaps fewer have it combined with charm; not merely charm of manner, but charm of nature such as Richard had.

The role of stooge did not suit him. Very quickly he was popping up with ideas, suggestions, contributions. Very soon he had worked his fat, quick, bouncing personality into a partnership in our team. But he was never arrogant, never impertinent, always loyal – though I think he muttered behind his hand at some of the Reithian restraints I imposed upon him. Quite soon he was constantly out on reporting assignments – not all of which were broadcast – and I began a private struggle with him over his use of language. He had then a positive enthusiasm for the cliché.

He seldom wrote what he was reporting, but rather recorded or transmitted it straight off his tongue: he had a rolling fluency in delivering it, but at a terrible stylistic price. I cursed him and slashed his copy and blue-pencilled his adjectives and cursed again and called upon him to think what language meant. In my pernickety sub-conscious mind I was demanding the astringency of a future John Freeman combined with the vocabulary of a James Morris. Richard went on rolling out his clichés with a relish and conviction that robbed them of their banality and positively gave them life. But, impervious to his real potentialities, I continued to try to shape him to impossible and inapplicable ideals.

Of course, the extreme condensation and economy of style required in contributions to those news bulletins were not his proper medium. I think he knew this at the time and was already working out how to transfer his resources of fluency to Outside Broadcast commentaries where they could find full scope: but he was feeling his way in the BBC and anyway was loyal to his team. Meanwhile he was most resourceful, as reporters must be, and reported all sorts of things. He sploshed about for days over-reporting some Fen floods. We went together on a rather stunty outing when a Dutch firm diverted a tin-dredger to have an unavailing go at the wreck of the *Lutine* off the Dutch island of Terschelling: Richard drove his car, which had cost him £3 and made awful clanking noises; we suffered a good deal of rough water and someone fell in; but in terms of news broadcasting the expedition was a failure.

He reported formal occasions with perhaps a whiff of his future carefully-judged style, aspects of the abdication crisis, of King George VI's Coronation, occasionally sports events, accidents, anything that fitted in to our requirements – and then, as my work took me more and more abroad and the cloud of war became even in England bigger than a man's hand, he reported military preparations, the end of the Spanish Civil War and Neville Chamberlain's return from Munich; and I think at this stage his style tightened and he set himself the standards of thought and behaviour which underlay the sincerity in his war reporting and his carefully developed technique of extensive descriptive broadcasting and television commentary. I do not think my curses had helped much. If he was tolerable, acceptable or a delight to later millions of listeners and viewers, it was rather because his charm of nature gave him a modesty which not only communicated itself to his public but furnished a self-discipline far more effective than the astringent requirements of his News Service days.

Fenland Floods

Richard Dimbleby's first year for BBC News hardly foreshadowed what he was to mean to broadcasting. But there were some signs of things to come that we in the newsroom could detect and appreciate in his early reports. On small as well as great occasions he already had a gift for finding the true keynote for each composition. He brought enthusiasm for the essence of each story and found words that blew a wind of change through BBC bulletin style. Perhaps there was still the odd newspaper cliché, but he was beginning to find how to convey grandeur without being emptily pompous; how to be vivid and colloquial without cheapness and without gimmicks.

Sometimes the signs of the future Dimbleby were particularly clear to see: in his reporting of the great Fenland floods of March 1937, for instance. Anyone expecting only another reporter on yet another flood story could soon see how significantly the dimensions were to be enlarged. For the first time – the first of so many times – he became part of the story himself. Knowing what we do of him some thirty years afterwards, we can read a good deal between the staid lines of a *Times* report soon after the floods had started: 'Contact between the Great Ouse Catchment Board headquarters in Ely and workers at various points has been maintained by means of messages broadcast frequently by the BBC.' Richard had, in fact, characteristically got himself to the heart of this network of control, communication and reporting. Here was the future 'anchorman' – a word oddly appropriate to what he was doing on board the barges in the floodwaters of the Fens.

There was something about his reporting of the scene that was also to become a hallmark of his work: the careful mastery of highly specialised facts. He did not deal in vague descriptions of 'hundreds of acres inundated in the grim fight against the encroaching waters'; he found out and explained in his reports what the complex situation really was – and explained it in terms of exact locations, comparative water levels, pumping-stations and sluice-gates, with proper use of technical terms: 'gault' as the word for the local clay to plug cracks in the banks, 'blow' for a breach in them.

To get the words, the sounds of what was going on to the listeners, Richard and his recording team had to cut discs in their green van and entrust them to the guard of a London-bound train. But such mechanics of the assignment daunted him no more than the future mysteries of Telstar. They were good reports to get in the BBC newsroom of 1937: I still find them good to read again now, with Richardian sentences like '. . . down the stream the moving pinpricks of light that are the lanterns of men working to close the cracks in the bank. . . . Perhaps at this moment you can hear the wind as it roars round us.'

When the House of Commons debated the Fenland floods, Richard's reports were quoted as an authoritative source for points under discussion. Another landmark for those days, but he was referred to anony-

Copthorne, Sussex,
26 June 1937

mously as 'the eye-witness of the British Broadcasting Corporation'. The name Dimbleby didn't mean very much at Westminster – yet.

In June 1937 Richard Dimbleby married a girl he had met as a fellow reporter on the family newspapers at Richmond, Dilys Thomas, third daughter of a London barrister. The BBC gave him a wedding present of £5. Had he been with the staff a whole year it would have been £10. The Dimblebys were poor and happy.

Charles Gardner soon moved over from sub-editing to join Richard Dimbleby as the second BBC news observer, and between them they covered all the home news stories, while Ralph Murray continued to report the League of Nations.

CHARLES GARDNER

Enterprise but No Faking

Richard was fascinated by the technique of the use of recordings. He was always experimenting with sound effects and with microphone placings. Here both he and I had to observe one very clear rule of the News Talks section – there must be no faking. To fake was the unforgivable sin. The bark of the dog that roused the household against a burglar had to be *the* bark of *the* dog and not just the bark of any other dog of the same species. We were rather proud of this integrity, and when it was suggested to us, as it so often was, that rather than put all concerned to a great deal of trouble to produce some sound effect or other, we could more easily and more convincingly fake it, we used to reply with great dignity 'News Talks never fakes'. I have some recollection of Dimbleby and Arthur Phillips spending all of some railway journey behind a new record-breaking engine recording the real sound of the train's wheels by dangling the microphone down a lavatory pan.

About this time there was the affair of the telephone boxes. This arose after a series of headline news stories had annoyingly occurred in the remoteness of East Anglia. Probably the Fen Floods was one of these stories. East Anglia was a 'Here do dwell savages' area on our map, because there was nowhere nearer than London we could use to play back discs for that night's news. So, after a series of problems about getting discs back from East Anglia, and losing a high proportion of them as Railway Press Packages, Richard had his telephone box idea. What was wrong with hitching an amplifier and a BBC microphone on to a GPO box and making any telephone kiosk an impromptu Outside Broadcast point? What indeed? So Richard and, I think, David Howarth of Recorded Programmes wandered around putting in calls to Broadcasting House from telephone kiosks and getting them recorded. In the end the GPO said the whole proposal was illegal and that was that. So East Anglia remained the great broadcasting waste unless, of course, one ignored the law and used a telephone hitched up to a recording channel at Broadcasting House and then remembered to remove from the disc the 'thrrreee minutes' interruptions from the trunk operators (before the pips were invented). Richard did this several times for straight eye-witness pieces, and so did I. We were never prosecuted.

Richard Dimbleby in those pioneering days of BBC reporting was cheerful, good natured, intensely hard-working and bubbling with enthusiasm for each and every story. Together we made youthful common cause against the hated 'admin' – the administrative people in the BBC – seen by us in simple black and white terms as the 'baddies'. 'They' couldn't properly organise the instant availability of a recording car; 'they' would hardly sanction the spending of a halfpenny on the news service; 'they' challenged the need to buy a pint of beer for someone who had helped us. Fighting 'them' became the joy of our lives.

With hindsight and the maturity of extreme age, I can imagine that 'they' were really scared stiff at the possible Trojan Horse they had invited inside the walls of Broadcasting House. The BBC putting out safe bulletins 'copyright by Reuter, Press Association, etc.' was one thing. Any allegation of error or bias could be neatly blamed on the agencies. BBC staff reporters were different. Might they not start to editorialise – to use the great power and prestige of the BBC to shape public opinion this way or that way – even by an inflection of voice? Outside experts might just land the BBC in trouble on this score, but at least they were not BBC staff. Dimbleby and Murray and I were staff and could not be disowned or explained away.

Richard and I were then perhaps too raw, too young, or too inexperienced to give these matters of high policy a thought. We never dreamed of editorialising. We were professionally-trained reporters, interested only in conveying undisputed facts and not concerned to hold inquests. Richard spent a great deal of quiet and careful time in ascertaining, checking and cross-checking the facts. If there was a discrepancy either he left it out or used the 'some say this – others say that' technique without advancing his own views. But – and this is my point – we did

With his wife in the London to Brighton Veteran Car Rally, 1948

this by instinct not by command. Of course we had views, but we never dreamt of inflicting those views on the public. Both of us had been brought up in the old-fashioned Scott school which said that facts were sacred – and the free comment was not our affair.

In the News bulletins time was strictly limited. It was common to be told 'You have 45 seconds in the nine o'clock and you can have 2 minutes 15 seconds at ten'. Richard's great and enduring strength, the ability to tell any story with a beginning, a middle, and an end in any stated time-scale from 30 seconds to a lavish $3\frac{1}{2}$ minutes derived, I am certain, from those early days.

The News Department was impecunious – and we ourselves were perpetually broke. I remember the night in 1937 when it became clear to Richard and me that there was potentially big news in the fact that Tommy Sopwith's America's Cup challenger *Endeavour* on her return journey across the Atlantic had broken her tow and was facing full gale conditions.

We decided to cover two key places: Southampton where Sopwith's motor yacht had now fetched up, without *Endeavour* hitched on behind; and Plymouth near to which *Endeavour* must sail if she ever regained our waters.

Richard and I tossed up for destinations. He won and chose Southampton. Then came the little matter of getting railway tickets. An office 'float' cash box existed for such emergencies. It was scheduled to contain £20 – the system being to extract some cash and leave a signed IOU in its place. We opened the box, and found a shower of IOUs – all of them signed by the news editor 'R. T. Clark'. So Richard and I turned out our pockets and dunned our colleagues – but the collection fell short of £3. Our next move was to go to the Queen's Hall opposite, where the BBC was staging the Proms. There we persuaded the cashier to give us £10 each from the till, on note of hand alone. Thus did Richard get to Southampton and I to Plymouth that night.

It was while on this story, and as a guest on Sopwith's luxury motor yacht, that Richard, replete with champagne and feeling thirsty in the night, drank some doubtful water, contracted paratyphoid, and was seriously ill in hospital. He was away for two months. The expense involved nearly broke him and he pleaded with 'Admin' to get them to pay his hospital bills on the grounds that he contracted his paratyphoid on Corporation duty. The story became involved because there was a simultaneous typhoid outbreak at Croydon at the time, plus a counter allegation that Richard had been negligent in using a wrong tap to get his water. Finally the BBC split the bill down the middle, but even so Richard's half of it was a serious problem for him. While Richard was getting paratyphoid at Southampton, I was getting seasick at Plymouth. I managed, however, via friendly pilots at the airfield, to find *Endeavour* and go alongside in a small hired boat to interview the Skipper – while Fleet Street was still arguing the toss in pubs ashore. I returned to start my own anti-'Admin' file on the matter of 3s. 6d. expended for a bottle of sea-sick remedy. We cleaned up completely in the *Endeavour* story for a cost of about £20. The newspapers spent hundreds – and missed out.

At this time neither Richard nor I could afford a personal motor-car.

We did, however, finally set ourselves up with a jointly owned Swift purchased for £10 with capital borrowed from Ralph Murray and repaid to him out of the 3d. a mile BBC car allowance for duty journeys. Richard and Dilys had the private use of the car one weekend, and my wife Eve and I had it for the other. I have now completely forgotten what happened to the Swift, but I remember Richard coming to me very excited to say that MGs would give us a new car each (to be changed every year) if we would put 'BBC News' on it somewhere. Imagine the temptation – but after a mournful drink, we decided that we daren't. My memories of Richard's financial troubles at this time are varied, but they had one central theme, 'Dilys has rung to say she is going to sell the piano' – but I don't think she ever did.

In December 1936, just before the Abdication, Richard and I were parties to one of the BBC's best kept skeletons – the day the BBC News Department threatened to strike. The newspapers, after Bishop Blunt's sermon, were now full of the Simpson divorce but the BBC didn't carry a word. Eventually this became, in our view, stupid and the staff of BBC News issued an ultimatum: either that night's bulletins made some reference to the main topic of the day – or there would be no News Bulletin at all. Richard and I weren't directly involved, but gave our general agreement. Fortunately the matter wasn't put to the test because that afternoon Stanley Baldwin made mention of the matter in the House of Commons and our local crisis was averted. Would there have actually been a strike of BBC News? I don't know. The key mover, Alan Wells, who was killed by a bomb in the war, felt very strongly indeed on the subject and he had much support.

Early in 1939 the Spanish Civil War (a very difficult subject from a BBC impartiality viewpoint) was delicately covered by Richard interviewing refugees at Perpignan. Later both of us went to Yarmouth to interview all concerned in an action off the East Coast in which a Spanish warship had fired on and sunk a Spanish merchantman and alleged blockade runner. I, and half of Fleet Street, caught a train to Yarmouth. Richard said if I would get the story he would liberate the recording car and join me. I telegraphed ahead and booked the only two station taxis in the majestic name of the BBC, and thus was able to isolate Fleet Street for long enough to sign up an exclusive interview with the Spanish captain for £5. I knew that, back at the station, O'Dowd Gallagher of the *Daily Express* was willing to offer £100. I waited ages with my story and the interviewee for Richard to arrive with the recording car, mounting guard on the hotel stairs and concealing from our Fleet Street colleagues who had now arrived that the principal actors in the drama were upstairs in the same building. Had O'Dowd found out he would certainly have outbid me. Richard eventually showed up (the recording car had been locked up and no one had the key, so he had had to break in the garage door) and we all repaired by a back exit to the Post Office where we used our car amplifier to transmit the story and the exclusive interviews. When we finished I saw a movement behind a pillar in the GPO – it was O'Dowd, notebook in hand, taking down our stuff. His office could, of course, have got it direct in London by listening to the radio – and probably did.

We enjoyed our battles with Fleet Street. We were handicapped by having no money to bribe or buy or to hire aircraft or boats, so we used the magic of the BBC name instead. For some reason people were very willing to talk to us for nothing when they were not so forthcoming to other reporters.

I have little recollection of Richard's coverage of the Royal Tour of Canada in 1939 save a picture of him gloomily telling me that even he who had a certain genius with BBC expense sheets was unable to account for some £96 spent on the Canadian trip and he didn't know what was going to happen. He was very low about it for days, until suddenly he showed me a memo he'd composed which said, 'You can't expect me to account for every halfpenny when I am with my King'. Apparently that memo did the trick and Richard brightened up again.

Indeed, when on a job involving good hotels and a chance of a grander life than either he or I could normally afford (I think we both got under £600 a year) Richard set about making the most of it. I remember him ringing all the bells in sight in one splendid hotel and ordering a manicure, drinks in the room, and expensive sandwiches – mainly I think to enjoy seeing the shock on my face. On jobs which permitted it, the best was only just good enough for Richard, and I envied the grand manner he assumed to match his temporary opulence. I suspect that this lay at the heart of many minor clashes with the 'Admin'. I hasten to add that these little assumptions of grandeur were done as a piece of gamesmanship against the BBC administration and always ended in a giggle of anticipation at the reception of the expense sheet.

War was drawing near. Richard was to go to France with the Army and I, as a qualified pilot, with the RAF. The fun days were over; but for both of us our attitude to broadcasting, to integrity, to non-editorialisation and to careful reporting, whether we knew it or not, was shaped for all time.

If I had to name those who contributed to the shaping in those pre-war days, I would say S. J. de Lotbinière of Outside Broadcasts, whose demand for professionalism and integrity extended its influence well beyond his own department, R. T. Clark with his casual but shrewd light handling of reins, Michael Balkwill for his sense of fairness and balance, and Ralph Murray's morning criticism of what we had perpetrated the night before. But none of this would have counted if Richard himself had not been the right selection from the start. I suppose he could have set radio reporting back for five years; instead he advanced it by a decade.

I first met Richard Dimbleby in the spring of 1939. I had been brought into the BBC to run the News Talks in German, which Ralph Murray had started a month or two before. Dimbleby was about to leave for Canada and the United States to cover the tour of King George VI and Queen Elizabeth. It was the first time that a Royal Tour had included a BBC correspondent.

Equipped with a new morning suit and evening tails, Dimbleby sailed on the 'Duchess of York' on the first of many visits to the New World. He shared a cabin with his father's old friend Edward Gilling, for long the

On the 'Duchess of York', 1939

Court correspondent of 'Exchange Telegraph', who gave him many useful tips on how to deal with the elaborate retinue surrounding the Monarch.

On this journey Dimbleby substantially increased his stature as a correspondent. In addition to being a broadcaster of enterprise he became one of distinction. Handling Richard's scripts daily, as I did at the time, one could watch his style mature and his national reputation grow during that Royal Tour. The Board of Governors recorded their appreciation of his exceptionally good work in Canada.

It was also significant that the King and Queen got to know, to like and to trust Richard Dimbleby. As they neared the American stage of their journey he posted a note (signed 'Bumble') from the Royal Train to his friend Muriel Howlett in News Talks.

The US looks like being pretty frantic. . . . We've also been invited to the Roosevelts' picnic and I have fixed up to say 'how-do' to the gentleman himself, which will be interesting. . . .

I took part in an amazing broadcast at Moose Jaw the other day, for the local station, and was announced with a terrific fanfare of trumpets as the star of the evening. They brought the mike right up to the train as it arrived, and all would have been well if the bastard (beg your pardon) hadn't got my name wrong. Very undignified having to correct him and say your name isn't Dunglehop. I suppose he must have seen my signature somewhere.

After that he had numerous letters from Moose Jaw, one addressed to Dangleberry. 'I think that's the worst.'

ROBERT ROWLAND

Visits to Canada

During a trip to Montreal and Quebec for the Queen's visit in September 1964, I spent a week with Richard Dimbleby watching the entire coverage of the event by the Canadian Broadcasting Corporation. It was only his second visit to Canada since he'd covered the journey of the King and Queen in 1939. Throughout the week he contrasted the mood of the two Royal Tours: in 1964 it was one of danger and hostility; in 1939 the Royal Tour was in the warm glow of Empire, when the Monarchy represented a great power on the American continent. It was the stuff of boys' magazines, when Toronto and Banff seemed as far as the Mountains of the Moon and when the coverage of distance itself was an adventure for the intrepid.

During a long lunch at the Chateau Frontenac in Quebec – long, because the food was good and the weather was fine – he told me of an evening in the Banff Springs Hotel with the pressmen and photographers covering the 1939 tour. King George VI and Queen Elizabeth had been with them in the earlier part of the evening, talking informally. But after they went the party continued and grew in volume of numbers and of sound, with Richard at the piano. As the day drew to 11 o'clock or so, the King appeared in the room and asked if they minded his rejoining them: this he did and the party continued with no change of mood or

style. A contrast, said Dimbleby, to the Mounties stationed above the Café de Paris and at every rooftop and naked window in Quebec for the present tour.

After finishing lunch, Richard Dimbleby took me through the heavy security of the 1964 Press Office and headed unerringly for the trestle table with piles of red and blue books on it – each embossed with the royal standard. 'The Book of the Tour', he whispered. 'Must get the one issued to the royal entourage: gives you everything – people on parade grounds, in processions, upstairs, downstairs, who the Queen is meeting, what time she starts on the lobster – it's invaluable.' He pocketed one, greeted every journalist he knew with the unique delight he reserved openly for everybody, and we left the hotel.

The flight to Quebec from Montreal was undertaken just for the day so that Richard Dimbleby could feel the atmosphere of this expected centre of French-Canadian hostility to the British Monarchy. He found the day totally rewarding because he was able to see the royal car, guarded by police and Mounties, on the quayside where the Queen would disembark the next day; because he was able to remind himself of how undramatic and essentially dull the Heights of Abraham are; because he discovered the names of the paintings in the Quebec Parliament Chamber, and experienced an overpowering smell of newly polished wood in the entrance hall of the Parliament building. And he saw the stunning colours of the Canadian Fall. But the smell was the important moment – and it emerged when he finally did his commentary to the edited film of the week's tour. 'When those pictures of her visit to the Quebec Parliament pop up,' he said, 'I shall be able to tell people at home exactly what was the most immediate sensation experienced by the Queen at that moment.'

Below: King George VI and Queen Elizabeth with Mackenzie King at Banff

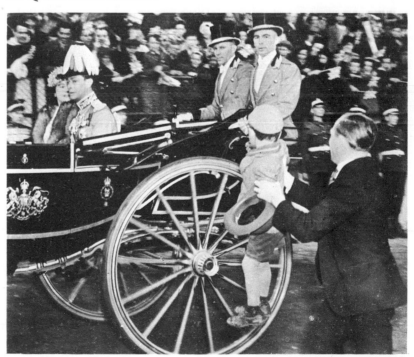

David Dimbleby, who had been born in 1938, was named after his god-father, David Howarth. As a fellow rebel Howarth shared the first four years of Richard Dimbleby's broadcasting career.

DAVID HOWARTH

New Ways to Present News

Richard set about reforming the presentation of the news by starting a kind of underground movement, infecting people here and there among the staff with his own excitement at his own idea of radio news reporting. I was drawn into it early because he discovered I was prone, like himself, to wild enthusiasm, and because I was in the sound recording section, which itself was new.

We had two mobile recording units, and Richard had his eye on them from the very beginning. Now, when one can almost put a tape recorder in one's pocket, it is odd to remember that the first of these units – they both recorded on discs – was in a converted laundry van, and the second, the perfected BBC product, filled a seven-ton truck and had a crew of four. Programme departments, at reasonable notice on the proper form, could book these outfits from us. What Richard wanted was to be able to ring up, at any time of the day or night, and rush off with one of them, then and there, wherever there was news.

The BBC was then not organised for anything so brash and spontaneous. It was nobody's job to go with him: so it had to start in an amateurish, unofficial way. There were six or eight of us in Administration and Engineering who had the kind of temperament it needed. 'It's no use asking anyone, they'll all be warm in bed. Let's get the story and argue afterwards' – that was his attitude, so off we went, usually after a day's work, wherever there was a shipwreck, a flood, a story of any kind that we could conceivably reach with the laundry van or the seven-tonner.

We drove like lunatics all night, recorded his descriptions and interviews, and drove again to the nearest regional studios in time for the next night's bulletins. I had a sports car which was vintage even then, and Richard and I often went in that, with the recording truck lumbering along as best it could: I remember tearing up the Great North Road in the middle of the night while Richard contentedly slept with his head on my lap underneath the steering wheel. And he was right: when we got the story, nobody did complain – provided we also did the full-time jobs we were being paid for.

There was one period when, for fear we missed anything, he persuaded Reuters to telephone himself or me at home, on alternate nights, if anything reportable happened. But that did not last long. Reuters night men never quite got the idea that we were tied to a lorry, and after Richard had been woken up four or five times in a night with items like a serious drought in Siberia, he let the arrangement lapse.

The cumbrousness of the lorries and their administration was his millstone. To BBC engineers quality of reproduction was all-important

then; to him the only thing that mattered was to get the story and put it quickly on the air, no matter how. He and I were both convinced that a simple recording apparatus, of adequate quality, could be fitted into an ordinary car which we could drive ourselves. Or to be precise, not an ordinary car: he dreamed of something fast and showy, say a Lagonda, with an illuminated sign BBC NEWS on the front of it, something that people would remember and expect to see. We even plotted (he loved plots) to have the recording gear made in secret and put it in the back of my car and broadcast its discs without telling anyone how we had made them; but that fell through because neither of us could afford it. It sometimes seemed hopeless to move the BBC, and at one time we tried – or plotted – to sell ourselves and our ideas to Ed Murrow of CBS, whom Richard greatly admired.

Nevertheless, by some years of lost sleep we did manage to cover a strange variety of events with those two recording trucks, and Richard's concept of 'our observer' slowly began to be established. I think what might now be called the break-through for this kind of radio reporting was the night the Crystal Palace caught fire. For us there could not have been a more glorious bit of news. It started just after the final editions of the evening papers: it was exclusively our own for the rest of the night. We rushed down to Sydenham in my car, the laundry van came in behind the fire engines. Richard with his journalist's instinct found the chief of the London Fire Brigade himself ('David, his name's Firebrace, life is perfect') and he vanished into the front entrance of the blazing building. I went in at the back, just in case he never came out again.

As the time for the News came on, we found we could not possibly get away with our records again through the crowds. There was only one thing – broadcast by telephone: it had never been done before. By luck, a BBC man much senior to ourselves had turned up from somewhere. He gave the authority. Our engineers disconnected the telephone in a café (I seem to remember that they wrenched it out by its roots) and tied our recording amplifiers to it. And Richard, hopping with excitement, black and wet and minus his eyebrows, was on the air direct, with the roar of the flames, the shouting and the bells. The broadcast brought out most of the population of South London to see the fun, and that displeased the fire brigade. The quality of the telephone line displeased the BBC engineering division. But Richard was ecstatic: the event had proved his point – that if we got the story, it didn't matter how.

By 1938 his ideas were fairly well established among listeners and in the BBC itself. We were at Heston Airport when Chamberlain landed from Munich with his piece of paper, and we recorded 'Peace in our time' for television as well as for radio. And immediately after we made our first foray abroad. An international force was supposed to be going to the Sudetenland to supervise its absorption into Germany, and the Germans gave us permission to go there too. So did the BBC, which surprised us even more. Neither we nor the international force ever got there – we waited in Germany for a fortnight or so – but I specially recollect that journey because the pomposity and false dignity of Nazi officials set a spark to the boyish naughtiness in Richard's character. We were met at the frontier by a delegation in vast Mercedes cars, led by a young Aryan from the Ministry of Propaganda. I see Richard being swept into Aachen in this equipage like a visiting potentate, dispensing Nazi salutes and Heil Hitlers, and then, alighting, clicking his heels and bowing to anyone who would take notice. Who else, at that moment in history – and with his physique – would have insisted that the man from the Propaganda Ministry should teach him to goosestep?

Far right: with David Howarth (left) at Aachen

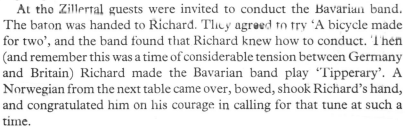

We went first to the Hotel Dreesen in Godesberg, where Hitler had stayed to meet Chamberlain. We thought Hitler was still there, but he had gone, and all we were shown was the Fuhrer's truckle bed, and the new green water closet Herr Dreesen had installed for him: the Fuhrer, such a simple man at heart, had been angry at the expense. Richard wrote a broadcast, tongue in cheek, about the Fuhrer's taste in plumbing, and we went on to Hamburg. Richard naturally asked to be shown the night spots of St Pauli.

At the Zillertal guests were invited to conduct the Bavarian band. The baton was handed to Richard. They agreed to try 'A bicycle made for two', and the band found that Richard knew how to conduct. Then (and remember this was a time of considerable tension between Germany and Britain) Richard made the Bavarian band play 'Tipperary'. A Norwegian from the next table came over, bowed, shook Richard's hand, and congratulated him on his courage in calling for that tune at such a time.

When war came, in September 1939, Richard was perfectly ready for it. He had won his way by then: we had an ordinary car, with recording gear on the back seat. A week before war was declared, he took the car to Paris, with two pots of camouflage paint, and left it there in what he thought was a bomb-proof garage. After the declaration, he and I, with Charles Gardner and an engineer named Harvey Sarney, went down Regent Street and bought ourselves uniforms at the BBC's expense. It was both emotional and funny when we appeared in them at Broadcasting House. Uniform was still unfamiliar, and nobody could resist a laugh at Richard dressed up as a soldier; yet senior officials were dewy-eyed when they wished us God-speed. We had our picture on the cover of the *Radio Times*, looking (it seems to me now) absurdly young and shiny, and we quite expected to die for radio.

But when we reached France, of course, there was no war at all. The British army was starting to dig itself in on the Belgian frontier, miles from any Germans. Finding no battle there, we went right down the

Maginot Line, into the wintry forests of Alsace and up the Rhine, begging the French to fire a gun so that we could record it; but they never would, in case the Germans fired one back at them. So we were driven to sending back strictly censored reports on obscure army units, broadcasting ENSA concerts, and arranging quizzes and spelling bees in which soldiers competed against their families at home.

We worked like demons at these rather uncongenial tasks. What drove us on, I think, was that we were on our own at last, with a vast field of broadcasting all to ourselves, and we were selfishly afraid that the BBC would send out a huge unwieldy staff and rob us of the shooting war when it really started. So we took on every job our head office suggested, and every one we could think of ourselves. The climax, as I remember it, was that Christmas Day when three of us – perhaps there was an extra engineer – did five major broadcasts, driving from one to the next on roads of black ice: a quiz, a church service, a piece in the traditional round-the-world programme, and two concerts, one English and one French. Nobody but Richard would have attempted anything so crazy, or been able to persuade his colleagues it was possible in one day; and I doubt if anyone else would have brought it off.

Again, it is the gaiety and the trivialities that I remember best in France, in spite of all the discomfort and the bitter cold that everyone in the Expeditionary Force remembers of that winter. There was a day in the city of Strasbourg, which had been evacuated in a panic months before. Richard had prepared a soulful piece about the deserted city, the dusty goods still displayed in the windows of the shops, the café tables still set out on the pavements, the abandoned homes. We set up our gear in a silent empty square, not a being in sight, and I gave the usual cue to Sarney: 'We'll start in ten seconds from *now*'. On the ninth

Left: with David Howarth (centre) and Harvey Sarney (right), taking leave of R. T. Clark, September 1939

Below: recording Indian music, February 1940

22

second, a jaunty French soldier came marching round a corner and gave a garlicky belch which echoed round the square. The silence, the belch, and Richard's helpless laughter were all on that record. I wonder if the Germans captured it: they got our car and all our equipment in the end.

And there were the horrors of phoney war broadcasting too, especially the quizzes, and most especially of all the one on Christmas Day. On those shows an army censor sat with us in case we revealed military secrets, of which the most carefully guarded was supposed to be the location of the British force. (Richard always longed to start 'Well, here we are in Arras', just to see what the censor's orders were – to shoot him dead, or smash the microphone, or what?) We put the questions to the competitors at home in England, and the quiz-master at home put his to our team of soldiers, who that morning were in a merry and unmilitary mood. We had prepared a set of harmless questions, but we listened with horror as the alternate questions came from London. 'What did Mary Tudor say would be found lying in her heart?' Answer: the shockingly unmentionable name of Calais.

It went from bad to worse: I remember every mark of dismay on the censor's face, and Richard's lucid comments whenever our microphone was dead. And then I became aware that we had only nine competitors, instead of ten. The tenth had fallen under the table and was being sick. Instantly after that broadcast, while Richard rushed off somewhere else, I had to eject our derelict team, admit a sober congregation and introduce a church service in the same hall. It was a day of splendid confusion and delightfully near disasters, just the sort of day that Richard thrived on.

King George VI with General M. G. Gamelin

But what I remember most of all is his influence on other people, the particular kind of glow he radiated, the sense of an organism much more alive than most. Thousands of other men will remember it too from that winter in France, for by the spring there were very few army units so remote that he had not been to see them – and there was nobody in Britain, of course, who did not know his voice. I cannot describe that influence, but perhaps I can suggest it. I saw him at that period – he must have been twenty-six or twenty-seven – with every kind of person: King George VI, the C-in-C, the old French generals of Maginot Line mentality, everyone down to the dimmest of privates in the Pioneer Corps. He was always himself with them all. And I remember standing with a Brigadier, watching him interviewing some soldiers. I said something about his ability to get on with all kinds of people. 'Of course,' said the Brigadier, with a sudden astonishing intensity of feeling, 'we all *adore* him.' That was the secret, I think.

In France Dimbleby perfected his broadcasting technique and his French. But he chafed at the lack of military action and envied his colleague Edward Ward broadcasting from the Winter War in Finland. In April 1940 he left by flying boat for Cairo and the British Army in the Middle East.

From then on his chronicle of war despatches reads like a history of the war itself. He now saw plenty of action. He entered Bardia with the

British troops and told how Italian officers and men offered to surrender to him. He went down to Khartoum, and was on his way to Abyssinia when he was struck down with diphtheria. He covered fighting in Greece and Albania, and a surrender in Syria. He lived cheek by jowl with German intelligence agents in Istanbul and was ambushed in Persia by guerillas. He travelled 100,000 miles in over a dozen countries, much of it in company with his recording engineer F. W. Chignall.

Once during the retreat back to the Alamein line their car stalled in deep sand. For twenty-four hours they had not seen another car. They took down the engine without success and Dimbleby decided one of them must start walking due north in search of a tow from some other British vehicle. He said, 'Chig, we'll toss up for it, and you throw the coin.' It fell to Richard to go and many hours later he returned with a tow. Chignall recalls: 'The real significance of this incident was that Richard, the army driver and I all knew that Tobruk had been retaken by the Germans, and that they had already put into use the transport they had captured from us. During the twenty-four hours we were broken down we were cut off from any contact with the British Army so anything Richard met could easily have been a probing force of Germans. I have always kept the coin I tossed that day.'

Richard Dimbleby himself described his Middle Eastern adventures in detail in that very readable book 'The Frontiers Are Green' published by Hodder and Stoughton. It is now out of print but available in libraries. This extract gives a sample of its flavour, and also of Dimbleby's continuing interest in surgery:

RICHARD DIMBLEBY

Watching an Operation

One night when the Germans were pressing forward and our tanks, guns, and infantry were falling quickly but methodically back, I was in a casualty clearing station. The battle was not far away; the noise of it penetrated the heavy canvas walls of the hospital tents, and occasionally a heavier or nearer explosion shook the medical fittings laid out in the operating theatre. The casualty station lay in the enemy's path. A sudden advance would engulf it and the wounded men who sat or lay in its wards. Several field hospitals had been overrun in desert battles; one, an Indian unit, had changed hands three times in a single day. The British doctors did not stop work nor did they have time to do more than glance at the German doctor who was using the spare operating table for his own casualties.

There had been some stiff fighting on the day that I went to the C.C.S., and a queue of thirty men waited outside the tent. It was nearly dark, and on the western horizon flickering lights showed the battle area. Bombers and fighters had been thundering low overhead all day, and at tea-time a Messerschmidt swooping low over the Red Crosses of the hospital had machine-gunned the wards, and missed. The evening lull was spreading over the desert, and the single groan of a wounded man sounded from the ambulance where he lay with his arms broken. I pushed back the blanket at the entrance to the operating theatre and entered the light trap that preserved absolute black-out. The blanket dropped into position behind me and for a moment I stood in the pitch-dark entrance, smelling ether through the second blanket. There was a clinking and rustling inside, and a voice. I lifted the flap and a beam of bright light shot through. In the middle of the tent three men robed in white were standing at a polished steel table. Directly above them a powerful bulb shone against the bright insides of petrol tins, split and flattened round it to reflect the light to the table. A copper steriliser was bubbling and hissing and letting out fussy jets of steam. An orderly in khaki with a gauze pad over his mouth was packing the sterilising drum with dressings. His shirt and shorts were the only touches of khaki; everything else was white and spotless. All except a long enamel dish on the ground which had a dirty leg in it. Someone had thrown a cloth over the leg, leaving the toes sticking up, blue and grubby.

I looked hurriedly away and caught the eye of the surgeon, who raised his gloved hand in greeting. He spoke to the orderly.

'Right. He'll do. Keep him warm.'

The casualty was lifted from the table and carried out, breathing stentoriously. The leg was also carried away, I presumed for burning, and the orderly began cleaning up the litter of bloody dressings and instruments. Two bombers roared over the tent. The surgeon, who was washing at a bowl of steaming water, took no notice. He had taken off his mask and I saw his tired, strained face. He smiled across to me.

'These battles are hell. That's the fourth amputation today and the fourteenth operation. I've been at it since eight o'clock this morning and there's a queue like Bank Holiday at the cinema. Get a move on Jenkins' – this to the orderly, who was preparing a clean mask and fresh rubber gloves. As soon as the surgeon was dressed again, the orderly lifted the tent flap and called in the next man. He was a burly tank driver with a field dressing twisted round his neck. He had been bleeding, enough to soak the dressing and stain his shirt. He came forward hesitantly into the bright light.

'What's the matter with you?' asked the doctor.

The man pointed to the bandage. 'Something went in here, sir.' He spoke huskily, his words wheezing out as though the sound were indeed escaping through a hole in his neck.

'Hop up on the table and let's have a look at it.'

The man stood still.

'Come on, jump up,' said the orderly.

The driver hesitated a moment, then spoke to the surgeon. 'I'd rather not, sir. I've read the regulations and I can refuse an operation.'

The surgeon stared at him. The man was weak and exhausted, his face showed clearly the strain of a week's heavy tank fighting.

'Then what the hell are you wasting my time for? There are fifty other men waiting outside. If you don't want treatment, get out of the way.'

The man said, 'Thank you, sir,' huskily and turned to go. As he reached the door the doctor called after him: 'By the way, you'll be dead in a week.'

The driver went on, and the doctor grinned at me. 'That always gets 'em. He'll be back later.'

Two bearers brought in a stretcher and laid it on the table. On it was a black soldier, a 'boy' from one of the South African gold mines. A chunk of shell had ripped its way into his back. He was conscious and rolling his eyes.

'Ever seen a major operation?' asked the surgeon.

I said no.

'Well, come up to the table and watch. It's quite interesting.'

I remembered stories of what happened to medical students when they watched their first operation. I could find no excuse for going outside. I moved up to the table.

The anaesthetist at the man's head was adjusting the controls of his machine. I tried to look bright and confident. I said to the black boy, 'You're all right now. You'll soon be better.'

He smiled faintly and gave a little groan. Then he said in a very low voice, almost a whisper:

'My mother – she'll be crying for me.' He looked at me once again as the mask was put over his nose. It was the look of a dumb, frightened

creature. I wanted to take his hand and say something to comfort him, but it was the anaesthetist who spoke. 'Breathe,' he said, bending down to speak in the boy's ear, 'breathe.'

The surgeon stood waiting. Presently the South African relaxed. The anaesthetist nodded and the doctor took a shining knife from the orderly. 'Here goes,' he said. I held my breath, unable to tear my eyes from the small patch of bare stomach that had been swabbed clean with spirit. For a second the surgeon held the knife poised over the black skin, as though measuring his stroke. Then it flashed. A thin scarlet line appeared in the flesh and a little blood spurted. 'Swabs,' said the surgeon, and packed gauze into the opening. Then he cut deeper and dropping the knife into a tray, held out his hand. The orderly put a few tiny clips into it and with these the sides of the wound were pegged back until it was a red mouth in the glistening wall of the stomach.

The man was snoring jerkily, and the anaesthetist held up a hand. The surgeon waited. His colleague listened for a moment and adjusted a silver wheel. He listened again; then nodded.

Somebody was being bombed; each crump shook the tent, and I could hear the anti-aircraft guns coughing. I thought the battle had come nearer. No one else in the tent seemed conscious of its existence. The anaesthetist and orderlies were motionless at their posts. The surgeon had plunged his hand through the hole and was bringing out various innards, placing them on the top of the stomach. I saw them through half-closed eyes; they were not so unpleasant. I thought of the shattered men I had seen in slit trenches and anti-tank positions. This atmosphere of cleanliness and perfect order was more acceptable.

27

The surgeon had his hand inside the unconscious man's body. He was feeling and probing with surprising energy, and talking half to himself, half to me. 'This bit of metal's got itself in an awkward position. Nothing this side – nothing over there but guts.'

As he explored, I imagined him back in Auckland, New Zealand, where he was one of the best-known surgeons. Now he was working as deftly and with as much concentration as if he were in a hospital at home. Thus he worked on every man brought in, though he was stiff with fatigue. No man did more for the army in the desert than this New Zealand surgeon and the other doctors like him who worked on the battlefield.

The battle continued, and against its drumming and rumbling I listened to the snores of the unconscious South African. I was standing close by the table, remembering how I had once wanted to be a surgeon, when the New Zealander exclaimed 'Here it is', and drew from the gently moving stomach a jagged fragment of steel. He looked at it for a moment and then without warning, tossed it across to me. 'Catch,' he grinned. I caught it; we always try to catch things thrown unexpectedly, even grisly slivers of metal with blood on them. As soon as I closed my hand on the fragment, I let it drop in disgust. It was warm and slippery. The orderlies thought it a great joke; one of them picked it up, washed it and returned it to me.

The surgeon, having made sure that no other splinters remained inside the South African, was sewing up an intestinal wound, balancing the torn organ on the palm of one hand and stitching away as industriously and as deftly as a woman darning socks.

'I'm just a cobbler,' he said. 'I spend my life sewing up holes in people. It's a foul job, really.'

'Will this man recover?' I asked.

'Recover? Good God, yes. He'll be up and about in three weeks and back with his unit in a couple of months. They're very tough, these black boys, and I've made a good job of him. Look, isn't that pretty?' He displayed the sausage-like intestine, neatly cross-stitched on one side. Then he pushed the contents of the stomach back to their proper places, juggling with one intestine that kept popping out of the hole. When all was settled, the orderly poured half a bottle of disinfectant straight into the stomach and helped the doctor to sew it up. A dressing was applied and blankets were tucked round the sleeping man. We followed the stretcher bearers out into the cold air and the surgeon came out with us. He had taken off his mask and gloves and outside in the moonlight he wiped his sweating forehead. I offered him a cigarette. 'No, thanks,' he said. 'No time now. Look at that lot.' He indicated a bedraggled queue of men standing, sitting and lying outside the big tent. At the head of the line was the tank driver who had refused an operation.

'Hullo,' said the surgeon, 'changed your mind?'

'Yes, sir,' croaked the driver, fingering his bloody neck. 'Can you do something for this, sir? It's beginning to hurt.'

The doctor pointed to the tent. 'Hop inside and wait for me.' The man saluted smartly and went through the doorway. 'They always think better of it,' said the surgeon. 'Funny how obstinate they can be. Damned good chaps in battle. Well, I hope you enjoyed yourselves. Good night.'

Describing Battle of Keren under shellfire

FRANK GILLARD

The Middle East Years

The BBC tried to maintain two men on the spot to cover the Western Desert campaigns and Middle East affairs generally. One was normally in Cairo at General Headquarters, and the other forward with the Army, and every few weeks they exchanged duties. Richard Dimbleby was one man of this pair for over two years, and for part of that time he had to tackle the total job singlehanded.

Of all warfare, desert fighting is the most bewildering. Few writers have ever described it adequately. With no natural boundaries to define the field of battle and to limit its movement, the action is liable to swing one way or another, and all too often it is impossible for any observer to say which side is on top. To this basic anxiety for the Western Desert correspondent was added the dilemma confronting the war reporter everywhere. Should he make his way to a forward position so that he could describe an engagement which he had seen with his own eyes, or should he base himself further back at some headquarters – Division, Corps or Army – at which he could be given frequent briefings on the changing position over an extensive part of the battlefront? If he went forward, he might well find himself watching a local episode totally unrepresentative of the larger action. He certainly stood a good chance of missing the most important story of the day, since nobody could tell in advance where the really significant things would happen. On the other hand, if he covered the day's events from some headquarters, he was wholly dependent on second-hand information. He had no means of checking the accuracy of what he was told. There were times when some of the information filtering back to these headquarters was sadly over-optimistic if not misleading. In either case the risk remained that a favourable picture one day might be completely and unpredictably reversed the next in the fluid circumstances of desert fighting.

In this situation the BBC man was uniquely vulnerable. Correspondents writing for newspapers were safeguarded by the fact that it was six weeks before their despatches were seen by the men whose exploits and experiences they chronicled. It took that long for a London newspaper to travel out to Libya, or Tripolitania, and in such a lapse of time news became history. A press report, overtaken and perhaps made to look foolish by subsequent events, caused no more than a wry smile when it finally got back to the Army. Many things would have happened in the meantime to put it into perspective.

Not so, however, with the broadcaster. It usually required twenty-four hours for his despatch, recorded on the spot, to be sent back hundreds of miles to Cairo, to pass through the censors, to be transmitted by beam radio to London, and finally to be broadcast by the BBC's short-wave services and heard throughout the Desert Army. When it was written, the story might well have sounded a well-justified note of optimism. But if in those intervening twenty-four hours things had gone badly, with fortunes perhaps reversed, there was little understanding on the spot for the unhappy BBC reporter. With some in the Army he became discredited, and sometimes confused and dispirited fighting men tended to find an outlet for their own understandable dejection in voicing harsh judgments against him. They are not too much to be blamed because they had no idea of the problems of radio reporting. The circumstances were inescapable, and the BBC war correspondent had to do his best in spite of them.

From Alamein onwards the situation was eased, because although there was severe fighting there were no more major British retreats. But Richard Dimbleby's years were the pre-Alamein years, when success and defeat alternated alarmingly, depressingly and often inexplicably. We were 'up in Benghazi for Christmas and back at Tobruk for New Year' as it used to be said. So Richard became the innocent victim of factors for which he was not responsible and which he could do little to improve. His reporting throughout was totally conscientious and honest. He never spared himself in his efforts to give as faithful a picture as his own very shrewd and experienced observation, and his sources of information, would permit. Those sources were responsible, even if they let him down at times, because he enjoyed the confidence of the top command. Yet in the end, by the summer of 1942, it had to be recognised that in his own interests the time had come to withdraw him from the Western Desert and bring him back to London.

It was cruel luck, because the tide was so near the turn, and it fell to others, myself among them, to report the unbroken success story of the Eighth Army in the Montgomery era. But Richard took the blow philo-

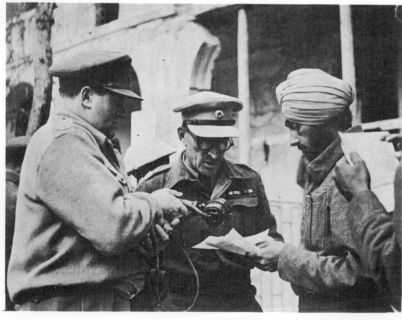

Recording messages to India from the Middle East

sophically, and, bitter as it must have been, he never showed his feelings openly in any way.

I was in the correspondents' room on the day when he returned to Broadcasting House for normal duties. It was a routine day, with not a single assignment of interest in the diary. The best job that could be offered to him was a visit to Salisbury Plain to report on a demonstration of Army cookery. The BBC's most experienced war correspondent, a man with a hard-earned and well-deserved national name and reputation, was asked to cover a story which would hardly excite a junior reporter. Yet he went off cheerfully, without question or comment.

This was the spirit in which he faced the two years of waiting, until D-Day brought him back, now as an Air Correspondent, into the forefront of active war reporting again. The prospect in June 1942 must have seemed bleak to him. Yet the period which followed was one of immense value. In it, Richard undertook occasional assignments of major importance such as his bomber flight over Berlin. During his spare time he stumped the country as a speaker in immense demand at armament factories and savings bond rallies up and down Britain. Most of all, he was helping to plan the BBC coverage of the great culminating phase of the war in Europe and to train the colleagues who would then be working with him.

S. J. de Lotbinière set up the BBC's War Reporting Unit.

S. J. DE LOTBINIÈRE

Operation Spartan

The BBC had told the War Office that the invasion of Europe would need a team of war correspondents who by their number could cover the frontline activity as well as Headquarters briefings. Newspapers were restricted by the tradition of 'one newspaper, one correspondent' in any theatre of war, and we were challenged to prove our case for a large team by taking part in a big Second Front exercise which took place in the Home Counties during March 1943 with the Code name *Spartan*. The BBC was to be allowed a team of correspondents on each side, complete with recording cars. Wynford Vaughan-Thomas, Michael Reynolds, Stewart Macpherson and Robert Barr were in those teams and so was Richard Dimbleby, with all his Middle Eastern experience behind him.

The troops were playing at war and the correspondents were playing at war reporting. Yet Dimbleby threw himself into his task and did anything that was asked of him. He would type away at his reports, putting them through censorship and making his recordings in the field just as though it was the real thing. Never for one moment did he make any of us feel that he had been doing this sort of thing for months and in the face of a real enemy. Nor did he ever grow impatient with the inexperience of colleagues, some of whom hardly knew how to put on a correspondent's uniform. Instead he added greatly to the success of the occasion by his good temper and wise advice.

As soon as *Spartan* was over the Secretary of State for War, the Commander-in-Chief Home Forces, the Adjutant-General and others assembled in the Director-General's office at Broadcasting House to listen to a selection of the reports from the two 'fronts'. The verdict was immediate and unanimous – the BBC could in future have its team of reporters and, moreover, the reporters were offered special training attachments with Army units preparing for the Second Front.

I am certain that Richard contributed enormously to the success of our *Spartan* coverage and in consequence to the world-wide reputation which the BBC war reporters were to earn for themselves in the next two years.

Dimbleby himself wrote a confidential report for BBC News analysing the lessons to be learnt from the Spartan exercise for the reporting of war in the medium of broadcasting. It was typical of his very practical and constructive approach to the problems of his profession. It also gave an insight into his view of a correspondent's proper bearing in wartime.

RICHARD DIMBLEBY

Report on Spartan

The Exercise

The exercise showed yet again that war correspondents are welcome among troops in the field. The Canadians in particular provided excellent facilities for obtaining information. With the sole exception of a few of the Household Brigade officers, I experienced no difficulty or unpleasantness whatsoever. Household officers always take longer to thaw.

The Team

In principle, I feel that the idea of a team in the field has been found workable, but I suggest one or two minor changes in the method of working.

Spartan has shown that the news observer with the team has his hands completely full with his own job; it is most unlikely that he will have any great length of time in which to co-operate actively with the Outside Broadcasts or Features man. The *will* to do so should be there, of course, but I do not believe that the speed of the battle will give the observer time for anything much beyond his own despatches.

In the past there has been criticism of observers in battle areas because they provide too much 'situation' material and not enough eye-witness descriptions. *Spartan* has shown that a combination of the two techniques is no longer possible. In this exercise, which was a close approximation to expected battle conditions, Force headquarters was generally seventy miles from the forward area. At the same time Corps Headquarters were unusually near the battle, while Divisional Headquarters were closer to the actual fighting than I have ever known them to be hitherto.

Hence it is not possible for the observer to visit Force Headquarters daily or even twice weekly for a basic general picture of events; he must concentrate on the forward Headquarters. This means that his daily picture can be fully representative of one or perhaps two Corps sectors but not, except in unusual circumstances, representative of the entire battle front. At the same time he can concentrate on the sector where the most important, and, in the eyes of the world, the most 'news-worthy' battle is being fought, and should therefore be able to provide an adequate and accurate daily picture for broadcasting.

This new proximity of formation Headquarters of the battle will bring one advantage. Although the observer will have to concentrate on the various Headquarters for his information he will be sufficiently in the battle to embellish his situation story with ample general colour; he will in fact achieve something not far removed from the impossible combination.

The pure local colour, the reporting of the incident, should be handled adequately by the Outside Broadcasts man, who should not attempt to give any general picture even of a battalion front. It seems to me important that the Outside Broadcasts approach should be of the 'here I am in a ditch' type; his report will then be found to spring naturally from the more general despatch given by the observer.

I suggest that the title of 'team leader' should be dropped forthwith. I am sure that de Lotbinière (who functioned excellently during the tricky conditions of *Spartan*) will be the first to agree that no one can be a 'team leader' while he is back at Force or Army Headquarters; nor should he come forward from those Headquarters or he ceases to fulfil his function of Liaison Officer.

May I suggest that his title be changed to 'Liaison Officer', and that in this capacity he should write and record with the static apparatus provided a daily basic summary of the whole battle situation gained from the excellent information room provided at Army Headquarters? In this way BBC editors will have the basic situation without colour or detail, for broadcasting or not, as they choose, and a livelier and more detailed despatch from the observer, covering the most important sector, plus an intimate running commentary from one of the interesting points of that sector. The Features man should select his material from the facts covered by the observer. In our case, Barr found this the right level at which to work.

I am sure that the above scheme outlines the best method of working, at least for maximum accurate coverage. It is also sufficiently flexible, as the Liaison Officer can provide at least general material if poor communications cause the observer to miss a despatch.

Communications

Here certain changes and improvements are urgently needed. At present the team has a truck and a car, but the Public Relations transport shortage which has obtained on all fronts since 1939 prevented our having a War Department car in addition. For the purpose of *Spartan* we used the static BBC car, an uncamouflaged civilian saloon which would in fact be useless. It is not reasonable to expect anyone to travel inside the Humber trucks. I know from desert experience what kind of torture it is to ride in the back of a truck on active service. A second vehicle (a *car*) is necessary for use with the truck.

The Austin saloon which I used during *Spartan* was grossly overloaded and rendered topheavy by a wire mattress spread over its roof. I doubt if its springs would hold more than a week or two on the roads of Europe (such was our French experience with the Wolseley in 1939–40). However, a vehicle of the type (i.e. a fast car or utility) is essential for the observer, whose whole efficiency depends on rapid mobility. The observer also needs a Jeep (for which I urge that application should be made). This would save time and petrol and greatly increase the observer's margin of safety and reliability. Instead of carrying the whole recording unit from area to area along the fronts, he could hide it in a suitable place in the Headquarters area and make his personal calls on the fighting units by Jeep. These fast little vehicles – ample for conducting officer and observer – are ideal for use well forward, and do not give offence to well-camouflaged Corps and Divisional Headquarters when tucked away under a bush or tree.

It is most important that the Army should *not* provide a driver for the Jeep. At present the observer has no driver problems and can move in his own way and at his own speed. Moreover he would have a spare seat on the Jeep for the Features man, if the latter wanted to visit a certain area with him. I think it possible that Public Relations will make difficulties on the 'no driver' question. But I assure you that this is simply because of 'establishment', and the red tape of regulations. Once in the field all difficulties disappear, but we must have the Jeep with us when we go.

I have stressed the needs of the observer because he, above all others, must be mobile. His job consists of moving from area to area and I urge that his transport needs should have special attention.

For the purpose of general liaison and communication it is essential that at least two despatch riders should be put at the BBC's disposal by Public Relations. I cannot over-emphasise the difficulty of finding formation headquarters during a moving battle. I believe that I have had more experience than any other correspondent of finding headquarters in action and in making use of systems of communication, but I have never known the job to be so difficult as it was during *Spartan*. To find a Canadian Armoured Corps Headquarters in order to catch their despatch rider may mean a search of three or four hours, which, as a daily proposition, is clearly absurd. The observer must have one despatch rider following him or the recording car, everywhere. This despatch rider can take despatches back direct to the Liaison Officer at Force Headquarters for transmission and return to a pre-arranged spot.

This is the only way of ensuring daily communication. I asked repeatedly for a despatch rider in the desert but could never secure one because of the general shortage. There can be no such shortage here, and I suggest that the BBC apply for two – one for the Liaison Officer and one for the observer. The first despatch rider can also be used for the convenience of the Outside Broadcasts and Features representatives and, indeed, it might be possible for the observer to arrange his des-

Top: the topheavy recording unit used for Spartan

Middle: the mobile recording unit developed after Spartan

W. R. Arnell operating recording equipment

patch rider's schedule to suit either of the other men if they are working in his sector. Such an arrangement would have to be determined by the observer.

Personnel

This is a delicate point that I must raise. I am sure you will want to consider it at your discretion. I feel that the senior engineers of the Corporation should be asked to choose only with the greatest care the recording engineers who are to wear war correspondents' uniform. At present they do not seem to realise that by donning the uniform, the correspondent is assuming automatically the status and most of the privileges of an officer, a status for which any soldier or officer-cadet must work and train. I regard it as an honour to be an accredited war correspondent, and I think my view is shared by the few of us left who had the privilege of being the first correspondents to go to France with the Army in 1939. We were the people who had to break some very thick ice and establish ourselves as trusted observers. We managed this successfully, and as a result, during *Spartan* exercise, I was continually meeting officers of Field and General rank who were friends of mine in France and the Middle East. But it is not enough to be on friendly terms with these men; to win their full confidence you must show a sense of military discipline and bearing.

I have learned how to conduct myself in the field and at formation Headquarters by three years of hard practice. Last week I was given as engineer and travelling companion a young man who had never worn a uniform in his life until two days before, and who most certainly would never have passed the elementary tests of officer-cadetship. He wore his field cap at a rakish angle and had a cigarette drooping from his lips from early morning until he went to sleep at night. He addressed private soldiers, military policemen and sentries as 'old boy'. At least on one occasion, in my presence, he addressed an elderly War Office General by calling at him 'I say', again with the cigarette dangling. He kept it there while he talked, and when he had finished he gave a friendly wave and turned away. The cigarette was still there.

I hope you will not suspect me of being a 'Colonel Blimp'. No one hates more than I do the unnecessary mannerisms of, for example, the Household troops. I am interested only in doing the war-reporting job efficiently, and I know from experience that we cannot succeed in our job if any one of us behaves grotesquely in a purely military area. Such people as that engineer will only be looked upon as oddities that should be better employed in an infantry battalion. We simply must fit ourselves into the landscape and conduct ourselves in accordance with the rank whose privileges we enjoy. It was a particularly embarrassing business for me as I know so many of the officers taking part in *Spartan*.

I wonder if you could find some way of ensuring that we have in a battle team only engineers who can hold their own in this respect. We must remember that in the eyes of the Army we are all officers and all of the same approximate rank. The newspapers are particularly bad in this respect, and personally I should like the BBC to set a better standard.

From then on Dimbleby had all the activity, and the danger, that he sought. He was constantly risking his life flying deep into enemy country. He flew in the first 1,000 bomber raid. He took part in the first air raid on Berlin. A German flakburst, only six feet away, almost turned the Lancaster over. The pilot did something violent to the stick and the bomber recovered itself. Dimbleby, who was prone to airsickness, was overcome. He pushed off his flying mask and vomited on the floor. The bomber eventually got back safely to its base somewhere in England, and Dimbleby pushed his way into the night express for London and the studio to broadcast his eyewitness account.

One seat was left. Swinging his bag onto the rack he dropped into it. As the train gathered speed two soldiers looked in, and finding the compartment full, stood in the corridor outside. Dimbleby was the only civilian other than an elderly woman opposite. She looked at the soldiers standing in the corridor, back at Dimbleby, and said, 'I should have thought a lucky young man like you would have given up his seat'. Richard was too tired to reply.

That incident and many others in his exciting and dangerous life as a war correspondent are to be found in his book 'The Waiting Year' in which he rather curiously called himself 'John Mitchell'.

The following despatches give something of the flavour of his wartime broadcasts after D-Day.

NORMANDY BEACHHEAD

11 June 1944. I saw the shining, blue sea. Not an empty sea, but a sea crowded, infested with craft of every kind : little ships, fast and impatient, scurrying like water-beetles to and fro, and leaving a glistening wake behind them; bigger ships in stately, slow procession with the sweepers in front and the escort vessels on the flank – it was a brave, oh, an inspiring sight. We are supplying the beaches all right – no doubt of that. We flew on south-west, and I could see France and Britain, and I realised how very near to you all at home in England is this great battle in Normandy. It's a stone's throw across the gleaming water.

I saw it all as a mighty panorama, clear and etched in its detail. There were the supply ships, the destroyers, the torpedo boats, the assault craft, leaving England. Half way over was another flotilla, and near it a huge, rounded, ugly, capital ship, broadside on to France. There in the distance was the Cherbourg peninsula, Cherbourg itself revealed in the sun. And there, right ahead now, as we reset course, were the beaches. Dozens, scores, hundreds of craft lying close inshore, pontoons and jetties being lined up to make a new harbour where, six days ago, there was an empty stretch of shore.

BOMBING OF DUISBURG

14 October 1944. I think that not only in the smoke and rubble of Duisburg, but deeper in the heart of Germany, there must be men charged with the defence of the Reich whose hearts tonight are filled with dread and despair. For the unbelievable thing has come to pass – the RAF has delivered its greatest single attack against a German industrial target since the start of the war – more than a thousand heavy bombers, more

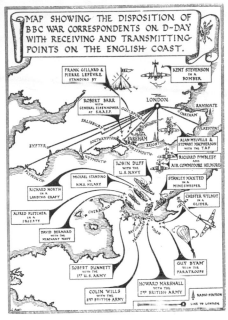

MAP SHOWING THE DISPOSITION OF
BBC WAR CORRESPONDENTS ON D-DAY
WITH RECEIVING AND TRANSMITTING
POINTS ON THE ENGLISH COAST.

than 4,500 tons of bombs – and it did it, this morning, in broad daylight.

At a quarter to nine this morning I was over the Rhine and Duisburg in a Lancaster, one of the thousand and more four-engined machines that filled the sunny sky to the north and south-east. A year ago it would have been near suicide to appear over the Ruhr in daylight – a trip by night was something to remember uncomfortably for a long time. Today, as the great broad stream of Lancasters and Halifaxes crossed the frontier of Germany, there was not an aircraft of the Luftwaffe to be seen in the sky, only the twisting and criss-crossing vapour trails of our own Spitfires and Mustangs protecting us far above and on the flanks.

The briefing officer had described Duisburg as the largest inland port in the world and an arsenal of the Reich, when he addressed the air crews. I saw Duisburg the arsenal, just for a moment, in a hole in the patchy white clouds that lay over the Rhine and the Ruhr. I saw the grey patchwork of houses and factories, roads, railways, and the dirty dark waters of the great river curving its way through the inland port. Then target indicators and bombs, H.E. and incendiary, nearly 5,000 tons of them, went shooting down; and the German flak, and a good deal of it, came shooting up. Duisburg the arsenal disappeared under a filthy billowing brown bulge of smoke. I saw no fires from our Lancaster – there was too much cloud for that – and I had one nervous eye on the chessboard of black bursting shells that had been superimposed on our fine clear piece of sky. But I did see heavy bombs, cookies, going down into the brown smoke, and more clouds of it pushing their sullen way up from the ground. Duisburg lay underneath the shroud; and shroud, I think, is the right word.

In case it sounds rather easy, this smashing of German targets by day, let me say at once that the pilots who are going to do it from now on are taking very great risks each time they set out on such an operation. The best they can hope for is a thick curtain of bursting shells through which

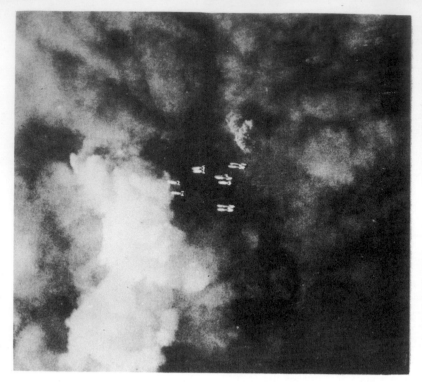

to fly, and the sight – the sight that we had this morning – of one or two of their companions twisting down to the ground in flames and smoke. But such hazards do not affect the plans of Bomber Command, that astonishingly versatile organisation that began the war with so little, and by courage and perseverance has built up today's striking force. As we flew home this morning, and saw a tight orderly patch of Flying Fortresses engaged on their Cologne operation passing us above the clouds, I could not help but realise that, together, Britain and America can now put into the morning or afternoon sky a mighty force of bombers that spells destruction and ruin for our enemies.

PATHFINDERS OVER COLOGNE

1 November 1944. Last night I flew for the first time with the Pathfinders, the force whose job it is to ensure the accuracy and concentration of the attack by marking the exact aiming point with coloured indicators – red, green, and yellow flares. The main force of bombers aims at the centre of the cluster of flares and thus gets its whole load of bombs into the exact ground area chosen as the target. This job of pathfinding, which is done by picked crews, demands a particular skill in navigation and, perhaps, a very high degree of determination, for the Pathfinder cannot let himself be deflected from his precise course as he approaches the target.

Last night our job was to replenish the flares already dropped by the Pathfinders ahead. The first cluster went down as we were approaching, red and green lights hanging from their parachutes, just on top of the great white cloudbank that hid Cologne. This was 'sky-marking': the bombs of the main force, now streaming in above and below us, jet black

in the brilliant light of the full moon, had to pass down by the flares. They vanished into the cloud, and soon the underside of it was lit by a suffused white glow, the light of incendiaries burning on the ground and the baffled searchlights. The flares seemed to be motionless, but round them and just under as we drove steadily over in a dead level straight line, the German flak was winking and flashing. Once a great gush of flame and smoke showed the bursting of a 'scarecrow', the oddity designed by the Germans to simulate a heavy bomber being shot down, and so to put any of our less experienced pilots off their stroke. There were fighters around too. A minute or two before we had seen the yellow glow of one of the new jet-propelled variety climbing at a great speed above us and to starboard.

We circled round the flares, watching the light under the cloud going pink with the reflection of fire and, silhouetted against it, the Lancasters and Halifaxes making off in the all-revealing light of the moon. Then we, too, turned for home.

Dimbleby was proud that his account of the crossing of the Rhine was subsequently chosen for inclusion in 'The Oxford Book of English Talk'.

OVER THE RHINE

25 March 1945. The Rhine lies left and right across our path below us, shining in the sunlight – wide and with sweeping curves; and the whole of this mighty airborne army is now crossing and filling the whole sky. We haven't come as far as this without some loss; on our right-hand side a Dakota has just gone down in flames. We watched it go to the ground, and I've just seen the parachutes of it blossoming and floating down towards the river. Above us and below us, collecting close round us now, are the tugs as they take their gliders in. Down there is the smoke of battle. There is the smoke-screen laid by the army lying right across the far bank of the river; dense clouds of brown and grey smoke coming up.

And now our skipper's talking to the glider pilot and warning him that we're nearly there, preparing to cast him off. Ahead of us, another pillar of black smoke marks the spot where an aircraft has gone down, and – yet another one; it's a Stirling – a British Stirling; it's going down with flames coming out from under its belly – four parachutes are coming out – one, two, three, four – four parachutes have come out of the Stirling; it goes on its way to the ground. We haven't got time to watch it further because we're coming up now to the exact chosen landing-ground where our airborne forces have to be put down; and no matter what the opposition may be, we have got to keep straight on, dead on the exact position. There's only a minute or two to go; we cross the Rhine – we're on the east bank of the river. We're passing now over the army smoke-cloud.

Stand by and I'll tell you when to jump off.

The pilot is calling up the – warning us – in just one moment we shall have let go. All over the sky ahead of us – here comes the voice – *Now!* – The glider has gone: we've cast off our glider.

We've let her go. There she goes down behind us. We've turned hard away, hard away in a tight circle to port to get out of this area. I'm sorry if I'm shouting – this is a very tremendous sight!

With engineer Bob Wade recording his 'Over the Rhine' despatch

40

8 April 1945. We had come into the German kitchen not to fraternise, that strictly forbidden practice, but because we had seen a large radio set there and wanted to hear the BBC news at nine o'clock. It took us some time to find London on the dial and the announcer had already begun the bulletin when we brought his voice, loud and clear, into the room.

The hotel family was already there when we came in. The old, white-haired man who watched us fearfully – I think the Germans had told him terrible stories of what we would do – his two not unattractive daughters, by no means frightened, and his grey-haired wife who sat knitting at the table. A woman friend was visiting them – one of the smarter women of the little town, with her hair caught up in a bright turban and wearing what looked to me like fully-fashioned silk stockings. They – at least, the women – were ready and anxious to talk, but we made it pretty clear that we had come in only to hear the wireless.

As we sat listening to the news about this battle area, I watched the reaction of this German family which had been engulfed in the fighting a very short time before, and could hear it going on now if we'd turned off the set. They were listening quite intently, understanding no English but catching the German place-names as Freddie Grisewood mentioned them. 'Hanover,' said the smart guest, 'they're near Hanover.' 'Isn't that what he said?' she asked me. I said it was. And then the Weser was mentioned and that being the local river, everyone heard it. Even the old man stirred himself from his gloomy apprehension. And then it was announced that the Americans were at or near Wurzburg. 'Wurzburg? Where's Wurzburg?' asked one of the daughters. The other got up and fetched a gazetteer from a shelf. She opened it at the map of Central and Southern Germany and the whole family pored over it, marked the places as they were mentioned.

And as I watched them, a thought struck me. This was a recital from London of our success, of the growing and spreading defeat of their country, and yet there was not one sound or sign of regret on their faces, no shock, no despair, no alarm. They just picked up what was said, checked it on the map and noted it just as if they were a bunch of neutrals hearing all about somebody else. And indeed, I believe that that's what many of these front-line German people are: neutrals in their own country. They seem to have lost the power of passion or sorrow. They show no sympathy for their army, for their government, or for their country. To them the war is something too huge and too catastrophic to understand. Their world is bounded by the difficulties of managing a country hotel – and there's no room in it for things outside.

Outrage

I have always had a feeling that the year 1945 was a turning point in Richard's life. It was the year in which he saw Belsen, and, as for so many of us, the world could never be quite the same after that outrage to human decency. And Richard was with the first party to go in.

It was a strange and frightening spring for the BBC war correspondents. We had covered the crossing of the Rhine, the last of the big battle set-pieces of the war, and the last occasion when we had to carry the microphone into the front line. I remember trying to do a commentary in the leading Buffalo assault craft as we plunged across the river at night, while next morning Richard was with the gliders that came through a furious storm of flak to make the biggest airborne landing ever staged by the allies. We met on the ground not long afterwards and I remember Richard saying to me, 'I don't think I want to see much more of war. I've had five years of reporting it and that's enough for any man.' I admitted that I had also lost my keenness for front line reporting – in 1945 the end seemed in sight and no one wants to take risks in the last minutes of a battle.

Besides, we were now driving fast through Northern Germany and we were beginning to uncover some of the grim secrets that the Nazis had been guarding for so long – party headquarters with secret documents of the treatment of political opponents, propaganda centres full of the mad fantasies of the Third Reich, forced labour camps with starving Russian prisoners-of-war. But so far we had not found traces of the most notorious of the Nazi crimes against humanity, the concentration camps, the mysterious places to which men and women were spirited away, where they were beaten, tortured, killed for the sole crime of being Jews, Poles, Gypsies, or for not believing in the mad vision of Adolf Hitler. We wondered if the stories about them had been exaggerated. After all, released prisoners tend to play for sympathy and surely not even the Nazis could descend to the depths these stories indicated.

Then, on an April morning which had a deceptive promise of warmth in the air, a rumour reached the press centre; our advancing troops had heard that ahead of them there was a camp at which typhus had broken out and they were pushing out a flying column, equipped with medical supplies, to contact the prisoners. Richard always had the good newsman's flair for sensing a story. I admit I thought the camp was going to be a normal prisoner-of-war one, and for the last few weeks we'd liberated scores of them. 'Nothing new here,' I said to Richard, 'I'll come up later.'

When next I met Richard he was a changed man. I spotted his jeep coming down through a narrow road amongst the gloomy pine woods that dot the level North German plain. There was rain in the air and the whole atmosphere of the place seemed dank, depressing. Richard got out and said to me at once, 'It's horrible; human beings have no right to do this to each other. You must go and see it, but you'll never wash the

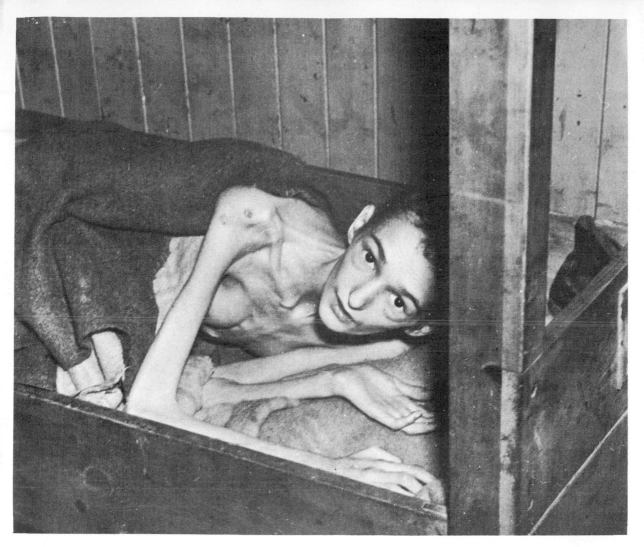

smell of it off your hands, never get the filth of it out of your mind. I've just made a decision. . . . I must tell the exact truth, every detail of it, even if people don't believe me, even if they feel these things should not be told. This is an outrage . . . an outrage.'

I had never seen Richard so moved. Until then I had always regarded Richard as a man who would never let his feelings show through his utterly professional surface efficiency. But here was a new Dimbleby, a fundamentally decent man who had seen something really evil, and hated it with all his strength. Did the memory of what he saw at Belsen lie at the back of his mind and give his commentaries on great occasions, his appeals on radio and television, a feeling for the suffering and anxieties of others which was instantly perceived by the viewer? I think it did.

I went on up that dismal road and turned down the sandy track through the pine woods that led to the gates of Belsen. What we saw and felt then is best expressed in the words of the most moving despatch Richard Dimbleby ever broadcast for the BBC:

The Cesspit Beneath

19 April 1945. I picked my way over corpse after corpse in the gloom, until I heard one voice raised above the gentle undulating moaning. I found a girl, she was a living skeleton, impossible to gauge her age for she had practically no hair left, and her face was only a yellow parchment sheet with two holes in it for eyes. She was stretching out her stick of an arm and gasping something, it was 'English, English, medicine, medicine', and she was trying to cry but she hadn't enough strength. And beyond her down the passage and in the hut there were the convulsive movements of dying people too weak to raise themselves from the floor.

In the shade of some trees lay a great collection of bodies. I walked about them trying to count, there were perhaps 150 of them flung down on each other, all naked, all so thin that their yellow skin glistened like stretched rubber on their bones. Some of the poor starved creatures whose bodies were there looked so utterly unreal and inhuman that I could have imagined that they had never lived at all. They were like polished skeletons, the skeletons that medical students like to play practical jokes with.

At one end of the pile a cluster of men and women were gathered round a fire; they were using rags and old shoes taken from the bodies to keep it alight, and they were heating soup over it. And close by was the enclosure where 500 children between the ages of five and twelve had been kept. They were not so hungry as the rest, for the women had sacrificed themselves to keep them alive. Babies were born at Belsen, some of them shrunken, wizened little things that could not live, because their mothers could not feed them.

One woman, distraught to the point of madness, flung herself at a British soldier who was on guard at the camp on the night that it was reached by the 11th Armoured Division; she begged him to give her some milk for the tiny baby she held in her arms. She laid the mite on the ground and threw herself at the sentry's feet and kissed his boots. And when, in his distress, he asked her to get up, she put the baby in his arms and ran off crying that she would find milk for it because there was no milk in her breast. And when the soldier opened the bundle of rags to look at the child, he found that it had been dead for days.

There was no privacy of any kind. Women stood naked at the side of the track, washing in cupfuls of water taken from British Army trucks. Others squatted while they searched themselves for lice, and examined each other's hair. Sufferers from dysentery leaned against the huts, straining helplessly, and all around and about them was this awful drifting tide of exhausted people, neither caring nor watching. Just a few held out their withered hands to us as we passed by, and blessed the doctor, whom they knew had become the camp commander in place of the brutal Kramer.

I have never seen British soldiers so moved to cold fury as the men who opened the Belsen camp this week, and those of the police and the

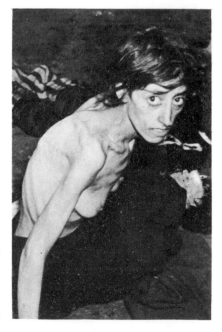

Return to Belsen 1965

The morning was wet and the clouds so low that they almost made you crouch under them. On each side of the road there were dense pine trees with cold mist in their top branches. Eyelashes and hair were beaded with moisture, and dampness oozed into the bone. Half-past nine and the narrow road was empty – just a cleft between the pines. 'Last time I came along this road,' Richard said, 'we drove like fools, because there were snipers on each side of it using the pinewoods for cover; they hung around here for quite a while. I think the turning is just a bit further on – there's a kind of humped bridge, I think, and then we go to the left.' The forests cleared and we turned to the left. After a few miles across the flat open heathland, we came to a small hamlet: just a few farms neatly kept, with hens and dogs and cows, children in gumboots, and red roofs that swept down to the ground on each side of the house like the wings of an eagle. A man smoking a cigarette watched as we passed in our big car, and then, by the side of the road, the place name – Belsen.

Past the huge military camp of Hohne, then part of BAOR, once the headquarters of von Fritsch and the Panzers with an Officers' Mess opened by Hitler; over more heathland we followed a sign to the Belsen memorial, drove through more pinewoods, and suddenly entered a car park which was empty except for some forest workmen playing football with a tennis ball in the cold rain. By the car park was the entrance to the concentration camp. It was an empty place, a cemetery in the middle of wild, silver birched and pinewooded country, the paths carefully laid out with well-brushed red gravel. Notices in different languages asked you to respect the dead lying there – about seventy thousand of them flung together in infamous anonymity. The shouts of the footballing woodmen faded as we walked across the heath to the monument. Total silence apart from the crunch of our feet on the gravel. And Richard said again: 'Do you notice that the birds don't sing here?'

'I came here first with one of the medical officers,' he recalled. 'We'd already been told as we advanced into Germany that ahead of us there was a typhoid area. I went with the officer to investigate, and we came here. It was a spring morning, warm and dusty, totally unlike today, and it was a scene of hideous filth and rubbish with a smell which had hit us long before we reached the gates – a familiar smell to us during the war which the medical officer and myself both recognised. I remember turning to him and saying, "That's the smell of death". But even that didn't prepare us for what we saw. This camp was the first of these places to be opened up and the report which I sent back from here caused a lot of worry at Broadcasting House. When they heard it, some people wondered if Dimbleby had gone off his head or something. I think it was only the fact that I'd been fairly reliable up to then that they believed the story. I broke down five times while I was recording it.'

47

We walked past a grave marked 'Here lie 5,000 dead' and then further on individual graves scattered in the heather – most of them marking the memory rather than the resting place of a murdered friend, son, mother or even whole family. Some were real graves, especially down by the woods where the women's camp used to be. But these were just marked 'An Unknown Body'. The trees dripped with rain and it was bitterly cold. In some way they were a link. 'I remember these trees. Emaciated people sitting among them in piles of rubbish, corpses heaped up over there, the huts down by this track, people in a state of pain, misery and hopelessness. The guards here were frightened when we took over. They expected to be shot at once, and couldn't understand the idea of a trial. One of them asked me if anything would happen to him. I was so angry that I turned on him and told him that he would be tried and I hoped hanged.'

Suddenly a weird moment: through the trees came a heavy roar like an aeroplane flying dangerously low. It grew in intensity shattering the damp silence. Richard recognised it: 'Tanks. That's the very noise that the people here must have heard when we moved in to liberate them. It wasn't a moment of joy, though, because they were scared it might be the Russians.' The noise gradually subsided as the tanks returned to Hohne from their exercises on the heath, and time folded up for a moment as the trees were suddenly peopled with ghosts.

Richard achieved the fusing of memory and emotion perfectly by two filmed statements. Every feature which we decided to include during our walk around the camp was mentioned, all in the correct order and nothing noted on paper: 'Earth, conceal not the blood shed on thee' – the epitaph of Belsen on the Jewish monument, a grave to a whole family, a square of marble laid down in the heather, the unknown dead down in the woods, some with small posies of flowers on their graves, the mass burial mounds of 800, 1,000, 5,000. And all of it told in simple prose empty of adjectives. He captured the silence, the mood, his own memories with a gift of style and sympathy which was matchless. 'When you come back after twenty years, you find the Belsen concentration camp almost, though not entirely, unrecognisable. Gone are the huts and the compounds and the barbed wire and the poor tottering people that were staggering about and the SS guards, men and women – they've all disappeared. The furnace where they hit them on the head and pushed them in the fire: all this has gone. And on a day like this, cold and rainy, such a contrast to the spring day on which I came here twenty years ago, there's nothing here but the desolation of heathland. All that you really find to remind you of this place, other than perhaps the lay-out of it which I can remember as I stand here now, are graves. . . .'

We spent four hours at the camp on this wet and cold morning. We walked everywhere, down gravel paths, across soaking heather, into the woods, stumbling over decaying boots and pieces of cloth and a mildewed truncheon. Apart from these fragments, the heather and the grass had reclaimed this evil ground. By the end of the morning we were as cold as the gravestones. But never once was there any complaint, and not until we were completely satisfied with the filming did we leave.

Then we drove away through the hamlet of Belsen to a roadside restaurant, and pondered at the irony.

It was a strange communion, this return of Richard Dimbleby to Belsen. The terrors of the place lingered in the trees, the monuments to suffering and courage were in every glance. A huge wooden cross stood on the site of the ovens. Wreaths, some of them five years old, some of them new, lay beneath it. There was a prayer written on a scrap of paper by a woman prisoner in the Ravensbruck concentration camp for those who were tormenting her. When Richard read it, there seemed to be a relevance to his own condition, to the strength with which he fought his pain, and to the way in which he lived with it. 'O Lord, remember not only the men and women of good will but also those of ill will. But do not only remember all the suffering they have inflicted on us. Remember the fruits we bought, thanks to this suffering. Our comradeship, our loyalty, our humility, our courage, our generosity, the greatness of heart which has grown out of all this, and when they come to judgment, let all the fruits that we have borne be their forgiveness.'

Dimbleby pressed on into Germany. He entered Berlin with the first Allied troops and was the first war correspondent into the prostrate capital. He broadcast from Hitler's chair in his bombed study, and acquired as souvenirs knives, forks and spoons with the initials A.H., which

Surveying Hitler's dining room with recording engineer, F. J. Cooper

he later provided at dinner parties for people he didn't like. He was also locked up by a Red Army patrol, and released after he had persuaded them that he was the son of Winston Churchill.

RICHARD DIMBLEBY

Berlin in Defeat, July 1945

As we would say, in British Air Force slang, 'Berlin has had it'. As a clean, solid, efficient city, it has ceased to exist. In its place is a broken-down, evil-smelling rabbit warren of craters, and hulks of buildings, and everywhere dust and dirt and squalor. It's true you can go into one or two streets and see no more damage, as you look along the side-walk, than you might see in London. But turn the corner, and again and again you come face to face with a chaos and a confusion that reminds you of those picture postcards showing ruined towns of the last war, the result of 65,000 tons of bombs, and the savage street fighting of two months ago. The spirit of the people has been shattered too. I've talked to a good many Germans in the last three or four months. And these Berliners are the first completely cowed and submissive people I've met. They've no spirit at all, only an instinctive urge to live, and that's not very easy for the Berliner today.

I'm not asking your sympathy for them, but there are certain hard-and-fast conclusions we can and must draw. Allied Military Government has got here one of the most difficult jobs it's had to tackle; all its earlier struggles in the Ruhr and the west of Germany fade into nothing when compared with this paralysed capital to be administered by three foreign powers, one of which, the Russian, has ideas and methods that differ from ours.

First, there is the problem of supply. Great quantities of food and drugs are needed now before the winter, not necessarily because we have pity for these people who are slowly starving, but because if we let them get any weaker, there will be epidemics of disease later in the year, and we cannot allow epidemics where we have allied troops stationed. There are already enough dead bodies. They are estimated in thousands. Still buried in the great heaps of rubble in this city and never to be rescued, enough for us to avoid any more deaths if possible.

Already the stench in parts of the centre of Berlin is nauseating and the city's water system is polluted. The incidence of venereal disease among the population is serious, and the German hospitals haven't enough drugs to give proper treatment. There's not yet been a major epidemic of typhus or cholera, but most of the population is in such a weak state that if an epidemic did start it would spread like wildfire.

For three months now there's been no refuse collection of any kind. When the Russians entered the city in April, they made each housewife responsible for the street in front of her house and this had to be clear and clean by 7 o'clock in the morning. That rule still obtains, at least it's still obeyed. When it came into force many of the streets of the Zehlen-dorf suburb in which I'm living were blocked with the debris of air-raids.

The woman who keeps our house – she was English until she married a German naval officer forty years ago – herself shifted nearly ten tons of rubble in ten days' solid work in two coal buckets. There's hardly any household refuse. She has very little to eat and wastes nothing, but what there is she carries to a communal dump a mile away.

There can be no doubt that the Germans, and particularly the German women, can be made to do everything for themselves. That is a reasonable burden for them to bear, but certain tools and material must be provided soon or they'll be too weak to work at all. Already they've abandoned the once regular practice of going out to the market a few miles south of us here for a few pounds of fresh fruit; the exhaustion of the journey and the wear on their shoe leather – people's toes are visible everywhere, and it's been pouring with rain for ten days – these things make the trip no longer worth while.

One other major problem still confronts us, and it's something that isn't easy to bring up, though no one here will be an honest correspondent if he ignores it, and that is the question of our relations with the Russians. They have fought a remarkable series of battles, ending with the savage struggle in the city which brought them their final victory. I don't doubt that to do that the Red Army needed the tightest discipline and the most rigid security; but now that the fighting is over, the security, if not the discipline, can be relaxed, at least enough to enable the Western allies to get on friendly terms with their Russian partner.

We must get on good terms. Without co-operation and some degree of trust we can hope nothing for the future. At the moment that trust is lacking. Somewhere between us and the Russians there's a barrier of suspicion and reserve. It's rather like trying to make friends with a fellow that you can't see on the other side of a high wall. Language, of course, is a major difficulty, generally speaking we can't understand a word they say, and they don't understand us, and there's strictly a

At the Brandenburg Gate,
Berlin, July 1945

limit to what you can accomplish with smiles and handshakes and nods.

After a week in Berlin and a good deal of superficial contact with the Red Army, it appears unhappily that the Red Army's officers and men are working to strict rules that have been laid down, and that one of those rules is that they must avoid too much contact with the Americans and the British. Perhaps we can hope that that rule is going to be altered. In a sense, of course, this racial reticence is understandable. We haven't been on particularly good terms with the Soviet Union for the past twenty-five years, and there's no reason why the Red Army should suddenly regard us as its bosom friend, just because we teamed up against Germany, but I do wish that we could make the Russians believe that in a place like this, where we're all shoulder to shoulder for the first time, we mean well and not ill, and can be trusted.

At present, passing through the Brandenburg Gate, which marks the boundary between the British and the Soviet zones of occupation in Berlin, is like crossing a frontier. There are no barriers at all, but you can sense a different atmosphere on the eastern side. You get the feeling that while you're tolerated you're not welcome, and you're not at all certain what's going to happen.

Let me give you an example of what does happen. Four days ago I went to Hitler's Chancellery to have a look round the Fuhrer's study and his private room. Now the Chancellery is in the Wilhelmstrasse, and the whole of this Nazi government area is under Russian control with a special commandant in command. I had lunch with him in his headquarters underground – a cheerful, friendly meal. We discussed the Red Army, the Russian policy freely and at length, and we criticised and received criticism in return.

Two days ago, on my way to a British military conference at the Victory column in Berlin central park, the Tiergarten, I made a through detour to see something of the Leipzigstrasse, Leipzig Street, one of the streets along which I've not driven. It's true that I was about two hundred yards deeper in the Soviet zone than I had been for lunch two days before. Half way down the Leipzigstrasse, I was stopped by a Red Army patrol with tommy-guns. I was forced to leave my car and go into a house, where I was locked in a room. It took me twenty minutes of strong language and fist shaking to get out, to get hold of an officer and to get freed, with the apology that it had been a mistake.

Now this was only an incident; in itself it was quite unimportant, but these mistakes are happening all over the place all the time, a continual succession of pin-pricks upsetting our relations and preventing us from getting them established on a strong and permanent footing. They affect everything, from the original movement of our occupying forces in Berlin, which was not accomplished without some difficulty and a great deal of delay, to the present movement of our supply convoys, and the conditions in which our special troops here in connection with the forthcoming big conference [Potsdam] are having to live.

But to return to the people of Berlin. There are two sorts of them; one whose orderly and ordered life has come to pieces, and the other who can get along whatever the conditions. I've seen them both in the past few days. The first was a detective inspector of the Police Department to whom I'd gone to check an address, knowing that the Berlin police had a secret dossier on everyone in the city. I found him aged and distraught. He waved to a heap of paper and cardboard blackened and dripping in his outer office. 'All my files,' he said, 'all my files burned black, no check on anyone now, no check.' And to him, the fact that the citizens of Berlin were no longer under the iron rule of the police was the ultimate disaster.

And the second Berliner, the other kind I met on the front doorstep of Hitler's Chancellery where a crowd of people were watching the coming and going. He came to me from a group of civilians. He was a Jew, with a briefcase in one hand, and he said: 'Excuse me, but would you like a tour of Berlin? To see the ruins, the Reich Chancellery, Goebbels's Palace, Gestapo Headquarters?' He rattled them off, and the price at the end, and as I looked at him I thought how for ten years in this city the Nazis had been insulting him and beating him, and how for ten long years they'd deported him and tortured him and starved him and gassed him, and here he was on Hitler's doorstep in 1945 when all his persecutors were dead or captured, and I wondered how on earth he'd stayed alive.

Some newspapers were sharply critical of what Dimbleby said about the Russians, but Richard quietly rode the storm. He was the commentator when Churchill, with Montgomery at his side, took the Victory Parade in Berlin. In five weeks he sent 144 despatches from Berlin, only nine of which were crowded out or rejected. It was a brilliant end to his war reporting career.

Then, after six hazardous and gruelling years, he finally doffed his war correspondent's uniform. With twenty other men who had reported the war by typewriter or microphone, in the Birthday Honours List of 1946 he received the OBE.

LEONARD MIALL

Resignation

When Dimbleby returned from the Middle East in 1942 he unsuccessfully applied to be sent as a war correspondent to Russia. Even in the middle of the war the BBC was already planning its post-war news coverage of foreign affairs. The small pre-war team of news observers, now developed into a great war reporting unit, was to be supplemented by BBC correspondents in the main foreign capitals. The reliance on news agency reports was to be finally broken. An announcement on the BBC's notice boards invited applications for possible post-war correspondents' posts. Dimbleby suggested that in addition to the coverage of diplomatic exchanges and international affairs as such there should be two BBC general reporters in Europe, who could fly at a moment's notice to cover straight news events, much in the way he and Charles Gardner had done in Britain before the war.

He suggested that one should be based in Berlin to cover Northern, Central and Eastern Europe, the other in Switzerland to cover the countries bordering the Mediterranean. He proposed himself for the second post. Unlike 1936, this time his proposal was turned down. The then Foreign News Editor feared that 'it would cut the ground from under the resident BBC correspondent's feet if Dimbleby or anyone else were given a roving commission in their territories for descriptive reporting'.

F. J. G. Dimbleby, Richard's father, had died at the end of 1943, after a long and successful career in journalism. Richard himself was then living with his wife and two children in the little village of Cuddington on the borders of Buckinghamshire and Oxfordshire. His uncle, Percy Dimbleby, who was the Managing Director of 'The Richmond and Twickenham Times' and the other newspapers and the printing works, invited Richard to join the Board. The invitation remained open.

When Richard returned from the war he was not wanting further work abroad and did not join those of us who were establishing the first corps of BBC foreign correspondents. He was however hoping for interesting work in the BBC at the microphone. He later revealed, in answer to a question from Daniel Farson in 'Frankly Speaking' in 1961, why he resigned from the BBC at the end of the war:

Farson: You had established yourself as a most successful war correspondent. Was it ambition that led you to resign from the BBC?
Dimbleby: No, no. It was the fact that I had to become a director of the family newspapers, coupled with – let me be quite honest – coupled with something else.

The then Controller of Programmes of the BBC sent for me and said, 'What are you proposing to do, now that the war is over?' And I said, 'I don't quite know'. I had hoped – because I was reasonably well known by then, to put it pretty bluntly – I had hoped they would offer me something which was interesting. He said, 'Well, I'm afraid we have got nothing to offer you. But we can offer you a place in the pool of home reporters' – which was twenty-five people who were doing the three-minute pieces all around with everybody. And I just thought to hell with that, and said, 'No, nothing doing'.

Now simultaneously with this, at the very same time, the family newspaper situation had developed and I had to go and become a director of that.

The BBC had very strong views about people being actual directors of things like newspaper companies while on the permanent staff. So it all fitted together very well. And I was able to say to him: 'I can't accept that. I'll resign,' knowing that I had the directorship to fall back on when I went out.

I remember pacing along a corridor in Broadcasting House with Richard Dimbleby in the summer of 1945. I had just returned from reporting the immediate post-war situation in Czechoslovakia and was waiting to go out to Washington. Richard was just back from Berlin. He was then earning £1,000 a year and was determined to get £1,100. The administrative people in the News Division had refused to upgrade him as a reporter. If he left the microphone and took an editorial job his ceiling could be raised. Richard was adamant that he was not leaving the microphone, and told me that with the family newspapers behind him he was going to chance his arm as a free-lance. For the News Division it was shortsighted parsimony. As a part-time freelance Richard at the microphone was going to earn far more than £1,100 from the BBC every year for the rest of his life.

LEONARD MIALL

A Freelance Broadcaster and his Wife

Under his uncle, Richard Dimbleby became the editorial director of the family newspapers. Eventually, with his mother's co-operation, he bought out Percy Dimbleby's interest and acquired the sole control of them. Besides the family papers, as a freelance he had the additional cushion of a three-year contract from Sir Alexander Korda to write films, though no film scripts were in fact asked for. But in the first instance his resignation from the BBC staff was a gamble. Television, closed for the duration of the war, had not yet reopened. Dimbleby's freelance broadcasting life started modestly with some schools book programmes and a regular newsletter to North America, but very soon developed.

He was greatly sustained then, as ever, by his most fortunate marriage. Dilys Dimbleby, as a journalist herself, understood the demands of his career, and from the day of their wedding in 1937 was a constant source of professional help and advice. She was also the only critic he trusted. She took over the management of all his professional affairs. She arranged his contracts, organised his diary, and negotiated his fees. On many occasions she also accompanied him on work both in England and abroad, *not only acting as a hostess for him, but sitting beside him during commentaries, organising his notes, passing him messages. In the early days of State commentaries Richard used to get letters from women viewers grumbling that his descriptions of the Queen's clothes were hopelessly inadequate. From then on, whenever possible, Dilys was there to jot down accurately – 'pale blue tulle' instead of 'a sort of light blue cotton'.*

They had in all four children, David (1938), Jonathan (1944), Nicholas (1946) and Sally (1947), and their family life was singularly happy. His secretarial work was done by his sister Patricia (Mrs John Haines) who spent two days a week at his house acting as his personal assistant. As Richard prospered he added to his roles of broadcaster, writer and newspaper proprietor those of chairman of Puritan Films and Film Partnership, chairman of the Commonwealth Group of Unit Trusts, and farmer. In all these enterprises Dilys was his active partner. She appeared with him, and the rest of the family, in films they made to demonstrate the merits of different holiday places at home and abroad, and she sometimes appeared in the television studio herself.

In July 1956 Panorama included a discussion based on the book 'Getting Married' published by the British Medical Association. In the studio Richard interviewed a doctor, and then an engaged couple. Finally he interviewed an anonymous witness:

Dimbleby: Now, one more opinion before we finish, that of a woman who has been happily married for nineteen years and has four children. You may perhaps some of you know her. I'd like to ask you if you'd give us your opinion now whether you think anything has been left out that should have gone in.

Married Woman: Well, I think the only thing that has been left out is something that really couldn't go in any book, and that's the question of the heart; I mean what is in your own heart really governs the whole of marriage, and I think that that you couldn't put in. But I think where the book fails, and fails dismally, is that it doesn't make a reality of marriage. It's rather suggested that if you follow the rules laid down, and if you follow the pattern set by the writers, all will go well and everything will be blissful. I think that's nonsense and I think it would be awfully dull if marriage was like that.

He then revealed the identity of his guest:

Dimbleby: Well, thank you very much. May I say that the last witness and I have been very happily married for nineteen years.

It was in the last five years of Richard's life, when he was suffering from cancer, that Dilys played her noblest role. During that time she was a constant support and encouragement to him and her determination and sagacity played an immeasurable part in his insistence in carrying on his broadcasting work as though nothing had happened. Throughout those five years she alone knew of all the pain and the depression that he suffered. She bore the burden of his illness with him and shared his public cheerfulness. In the last three months of his life Dilys was constantly with him, often staying the night at the hospital and always there eighteen hours a day, helping to

At Danley Farm, nurse him, encouraging him, and talking to him about plans for the future.
Lynchmere, Surrey, with She was a wife he deserved.
Nicholas, Jonathan,   As managing director of the 'Richmond and Twickenham Times' group
Sally, David of newspapers Richard Dimbleby was a model employer. The General
Secretary of the Printing and Kindred Trades Federation recalls:

GRANVILLE EASTWOOD

A Truly Human Employer

From the start he took a practical interest in the welfare of his employees. When they were ill, he wrote to them personally, sent them
fruit and flowers, and on appropriate occasions made specialist treatment available. In a score of ways he showed that he cared. For
instance, he arranged for the Italian-born wife of one of his employees
who was seriously ill to visit her homeland along with her four children,
and after she died he continued to take a helpful interest in the family.
    When, very soon after he took control of the paper, Mr Dimbleby
learned that a retiring employee – to whom he was making a presenta-

tion – would not be receiving a pension from the firm, he not only put the matter right but instituted a contributory pension scheme. Later he subsidised a fund so that employees did not lose financially when away sick. Shocked when two of his men died suddenly, he organised free life insurance so that the widows of those with three or more years service would receive £1,000.

My first meeting with Mr Dimbleby was in 1959 when I appeared on *Panorama* in a programme dealing with a national printing and newspaper dispute involving a claim for a forty-hour week. He made very clear to me in conversation his sympathy with our unions' struggle for better conditions and he introduced the shorter working week into his firm in advance of the conclusion of negotiations. Later, when a national agreement for a third week's holiday was reached, Mr Dimbleby not only most readily operated the terms of the settlement but gave even longer holidays to his employees.

In these and many other ways, Mr Dimbleby made sure that a share of the results of the success of his newspapers was passed on to his employees. The printing trade unions will always remember with gratitude the example he set as an employer and the lead he gave to the industry. I am sure that, so far as his newspaper activities are concerned, Mr Dimbleby would ask for no better tribute than that just paid to him by his staff who have described him as 'a friend and truly human employer'.

Another example of his personal kindness was recalled in a letter to the 'Daily Mirror' dictated by Una Byfields:

Few people may know personally how kind Richard Dimbleby was, but I do. I have been a patient in hospital since I was ten – I am now forty-three – and I am disabled.

For the past three or four years Mr Dimbleby has sent money so that I could have a lovely holiday at a Caister-on-Sea holiday camp. He came down and made us happy and took me out in the car and he wrote to me in hospital.

All the patients who go to the camp will miss him very much indeed. He was a grand gentleman.

LEONARD MIALL

First Major Television Commentary

The BBC opened the world's first public television service in November 1936, a few weeks after Richard Dimbleby reported for duty at Broadcasting House. He was interested in the new medium, and even before the war had sent to the first Director of Television, Gerald Cock, a plan for televising news and topical events. He had also had one experience as a television commentator. His description of Chamberlain's return from Munich with 'Peace in our time' in 1938 had been carried on television as well as radio.

But the BBC's sole television transmitter mast at Alexandra Palace would have made a perfect direction finder for enemy aircraft, and tele-

58

vision had had to close for the duration. The staff and equipment were widely dispersed, so it was not planned to restart the service until 7 June 1946, the eve of the great Victory March through London.

As soon as Dimbleby heard the date he wrote to the genial Irishman in charge of post-war television, Maurice Gorham.

'Have you a vacancy for a commentator on Victory Day?' he asked. 'My film contract and my writing leave me the master of my time. You'll know, of course, that I've done a good many major commentary jobs for Sound O.B.s and I think I understand the different technique for your medium.'

In fact the job had just been promised to Freddie Grisewood, who had had much more pre-war television experience than Dimbleby. But he was happily accepted as a second string. Ian Orr-Ewing, who was then the manager of television outside broadcasts, commented: 'I think it should be made clear to Dimbleby that Grisewood would have to be responsible for leading, and stopping any tendency of Dimbleby's to lapse into a "sound" commentary'.

So Dimbleby got his first post-war television job as a commentator on a state occasion. Television reopened for under 100,000 viewers who still had their pre-war sets. The first and only outside broadcast unit, originally used for King George VI's Coronation, was refurbished and brought back into action. For those interested in both history and television technicalities, Camera 1 was an ordinary Emitron camera with a 12" lens, to give a maximum view down the Mall, Camera 2 was a Super-Emitron with a 20" lens to take close-ups of the King, Mr Attlee and Mr Churchill, and Camera 3 was a second Super-Emitron with a 6" lens which took a mid-shot of the columns marching past.

Gorham warned the Controller of Engineering, Harold Bishop, that the gear was still shaky, and sought his help in keeping out VIPs who might want to inspect the unit in the Mall, diagonally opposite King George VI's reviewing stand. Bishop replied, 'I will do my best to dissuade visitors, "very important" and otherwise, from going to see the television outside broadcast unit. But even television outside broadcasts can hardly expect to work in a vacuum and even they may have to put up with a few tiresome people like myself, if I feel it is part of my job to pay them a visit!'

Dimbleby was to get to know this problem well. The television equipment, and his own familiar ample figure, would always draw a crowd. He was invariably courteous, and drew the line only at bystanders actually interfering with operations, or demanding autographs during a meal.

Dimbleby's first post-war outside broadcast was a success, although the picture monitor gave trouble (this was to recur many times in his career) and he complained that the commentary box was the Black Hole of Calcutta. The new television commentator at a major state event had established himself.

Alas, a second television programme planned for the evening of Victory Day was a total failure. Television cables had been laid in advance so that the only outside broadcast unit could leave the Mall immediately after the parade, and park in Victoria Gardens alongside the House of Commons to cover the aquatic display in the Thames.

The weather was so awful that the camera cables would no longer work, and Victoria Gardens were completely under water. Ian Orr-Ewing, later to become a Conservative Minister, wrote on 14 June 1946 to the Lord Great Chamberlain's office to apologise, saying, 'I hope that we shall have a chance at a later date of doing a programme from the Houses of Parliament as I think they will provide most interesting television material.'

Television had to wait twelve years before it was allowed (with Richard Dimbleby as commentator) to enter the House of Lords.

The problem for a television speaker of avoiding 'lapsing into a "sound" commentary' was one which Dimbleby thoroughly understood. Later he put it thus:

'To turn to television, a good radio commentator must work to a carefully prearranged plan with his producer, for he is no longer his own master, and subordinate himself to the televised picture. In short, he must become an annotator rather than a commentator.'

Stuart Hood, who had been Controller of Programmes for BBC Television and later for Rediffusion Television, analysed this problem in an article which he wrote in the 'Spectator' just after Dimbleby's death:

STUART HOOD

Everyman

Richard Dimbleby was one of the few men who, having made their names as radio commentators or correspondents – often in the trials and dangers of war, were able to effect the difficult transition to television. The obstacles they encountered in adapting themselves to the new medium were partly technical. When working in radio they had become used to seeing for the listener. The art of seeing for others rests on great verbal fluency – the ability, in particular, to keep up an unbroken stream of detailed visual images, to supplement the fragments of sound conveyed to the listener by the microphone. In the case of television, the commentator sees *with* the viewer. His role is radically different. He is there to nudge him into attention – to make sure that he does not miss some point of interest, to help him to focus, to create expectancy, and to give coherence to the images on the television screen. Unlike his radio colleague, he must know the value of silence and how to use it during those seconds or minutes when the pictures speak for themselves. This technique Dimbleby set himself to master, taking over into television, however, the habit of detailed preparation, of thorough briefing, he had

Lord Mayor's Show, 1948

learned in radio. In time he became one of the acknowledged masters of the art, known and respected throughout the profession, in Europe, in the United States, a virtuoso who will not easily be replaced.

But all the facility in the world, all the verbal tact, the agile memory, would have been useless had he not also been an impressive figure in front of the camera, which with its capricious electronic eye can diminish some men, caricature others, and by adding a face to a voice rob words of their power and authority. Dimbleby had the great good fortune to photograph well. He had, moreover, a presence which had something to do with his physical bulk, with the comfortable way he settled himself into his chair at the beginning of a long spell on election nights, with the way he moved about in a cluttered studio with the surprising surefooted-ness of a large, familiar animal. He had, too, a *persona* which was at once attractive and reassuring. A *persona* may, in its literal translation, be a mask – a public face put on for public occasion, carefully cultivated, art-fully built up over the years. Or it can be the true outward physical expression of a man or woman's personality. Dimbleby's *persona* was such an emanation. He was as he looked. As he thought and felt, he spoke. He had only to be himself to reassure his audience, to convince them of the importance of what they were to see and hear, to make them receptive and interested.

Inevitably he had his critics who felt that he was altogether too reassur-ing, too much the embodiment of accepted values and traditional loyal-ties. They heard him drop his voice in the Abbey or on some royal occasion and spoke of his obsequiousness. There may have been some-thing in the first charge, but the second does not stand up to analysis. If he dropped his voice, it was usually for a good reason – not to let it in-trude on an event, often of a religious or ceremonial nature, of which he was only an observer. As to his being a traditionalist, it was true in the sense that his views and sentiments were echoed by the generality of the citizens of this country. He was a kind of Everyman, the voice and per-sonification of thoughts and emotions no less deeply felt or less real for being either mute or inadequately formulated. An institution like the BBC, charged under the terms of its charter to function as a public ser-vice, requires such a personality; which does not mean that it should not also have its mockers, its voices of dissent and disrespect crying out that the emperor has no clothes.

The relationship between a television personality and his audience is not one-sided. The viewers are not merely passive lumps of receptivity. Over the years he establishes a nexus with them. A kind of dialogue springs up between the viewer and performer. The question is: On what level does the dialogue take place? Hence the extreme importance of the man a television organisation chooses as its main commentator. It is the need to sustain this dialogue which lays such a great responsibility on the man himself. It is easy enough to think of television personalities who do little else but reinforce ignorance and triviality, pander to petty greed, or strengthen the ignorant in their prejudices. Dimbleby did none of these things. He spoke to his viewers in terms of decency, of human feel-ing and, on occasion, of righteous indignation. There is a phrase much used and misused in the television profession. It is 'to identify'. I believe it to be a legitimate use of the verb to say that the viewers 'identified' with Dimbleby and in so doing learned to find and develop in themselves those human and public qualities which were his by nature and education – tolerance, a certain *gravitas* relieved by a sense of humour, concern for others, dislike of cruelty and indifference, a belief that emotion is, when genuine, nothing to be ashamed of. The BBC was fortunate in having such a man to serve it. The viewers were lucky in having him to speak with and for them.

Charles Collingwood, now Chief European Correspondent of the Columbia Broadcasting System, was a fellow war correspondent with Richard Dimbleby throughout World War II. He knows at first hand the problems of the television performer.

CHARLES COLLINGWOOD

Isolated in a Pool of Light

I remember running into Richard Dimbleby at the front in France in 1944. He was carrying with him a new and highly ingenious portable disc recording device which the BBC engineers had just developed. It was the latest thing and he demonstrated it to me with the greatest enthusiasm, tilting it alarmingly on one side as he talked into the microphone, bouncing it up and down as he recorded, and then playing it back triumphantly. He showed me the tiny motor, the miniature gears that kept the speed constant in every position, the way the recording head was cushioned against shock. He knew all about it and exactly how it worked. My own more primitive American instrument remained a complete mystery to me and I had to be accompanied by an expert to operate it. Richard handled his himself.

As we advanced into the increasing complications of television, Dimbleby remained abreast of the developing technology. He knew what every lens could do, the limitations of the image orthicon tube, the importance of lighting. Because of this, he knew what was likely to go wrong. This is an inestimable advantage to a broadcaster who stands there in his pool of light, with all the public responsibility for the programme on his shoulders, yet as isolated from the technical infrastructure which keeps him on the air as if he were in a diving bell. When something goes wrong, unless he knows what must have happened, he is lost, pitifully burbling and complaining in public view until it is put right. But Dimbleby could always guess what had happened and his rescues of broadcasts from technical difficulties became legendary. His famous aplomb was solidly based on professional understanding of the medium.

All this made him a joy to work with. Technical crews in America as well as in the BBC always liked to be assigned to a Dimbleby programme, and his obvious expertise was a great comfort to those who found themselves being interviewed by him on his programmes. A television interview can be a frightening experience, but Dimbleby was so obviously in command that his presence was very reassuring to the fellow in the other chair. He wasn't particularly famous for it, but I always thought

Dimbleby was a superb interviewer. His style of courteous persistence and the rapport he established with his guests often brought out a truer picture of his subjects than the more abrasive and challenging style of other interviewers which, by putting the subject on the defensive, tends to elicit only defensive reactions.

As it happened, we did a good many transatlantic broadcasts together when Telstar and Early Bird appeared in the heavens. He understood all about them, too. It was a great relief to know that he would be on the other end of these celestial communications, for if anything went wrong you could be sure that with Dimbleby there it would not be irretrievable. These broadcasts brought him more regularly before American audiences. He was the only British broadcaster who was immediately identifiable to large numbers of Americans. This is not surprising; Americans pride themselves on their ability to recognise the real thing.

Richard Dimbleby was the real thing, all right – both as a person and broadcaster. His influence upon the techniques of broadcasting was very great. Because he knew his job so well, he forced others to learn theirs. I'm sorry he won't be around to see all the new developments in television. He would have been able to understand them completely and perhaps, thereby, make some of the rest of us understand them a little.

Telstar Programme from CBS, New York, with Walter Cronkite

Dimbleby gave his own views on the technique of interviewing, whether on television or radio, when he was the guest of Asian Club:

RICHARD DIMBLEBY

On Interviewing

You must be interested in people. You must want to get out of them the information you're trying to get and you must be, I think, good at listening to people.

There's one other thing I think which an interviewer needs to be able to do, and that is to control an interview without it being apparent to the

With a French diver

With Dr Robert Stopford,
Bishop of London

Down Your Way:
Romney, Hythe and
Dymchurch Railway

other person that he's doing so. That is to say, if you have an interview which is going to last five minutes, and you know the various things you're thinking of asking, the person whom you're interviewing probably doesn't realise as well as you do, if you're a professional broadcaster, how long five minutes is. You know, after years you get to know exactly, how long a certain time is, just in your head. If they don't know, and they may go off into some long, long story which takes much longer than it ought to take, you have got to be able to get them off this story, bring them on to the next thing you want to ask them, get them quickly through that and stop the whole thing in the right time without anybody noticing that you've been pushing and pulling the person to whom you're talking. This is a small thing but it's quite important.

Dimbleby perfected his interviewing skill, and also his abiding knowledge of his own country, through his appearances on the radio programme Down Your Way which he made every week until 1953. He was prepared to go anywhere and do anything. John Shuter was his producer:

JOHN SHUTER

Down Your Way

The time was two o'clock in the morning. Richard Dimbleby was seated comfortably on what he had just described as the 'hot seat'. In fact this was the live rail in one of the London Underground Railway tunnels hundreds of feet below Regent's Park. Although the current was of course turned off, Richard insisted on exciting my imagination with delightful little word pictures conjuring up visions of a man at the sub-station miles away with his hand on the circuit breaker unwittingly about to switch on! We were recording a programme about the night workers of London. One of them described herself as a 'fluffer'. In simple language this meant that her job was to clean the tunnels through which the trains thundered all day. Richard was so amused by this title that he asked me to try to include someone with an unusually titled job in each week's programme.

This was a somewhat tall order, though we did eventually assemble quite an assortment from the lady 'fluffer' to a lady 'white hot rivet catcher' in a Newcastle shipyard, and including a Bradford family whose window sign advertised their occupation as 'family rat catchers authorised by the Ministry of Food'. Throughout this recording the entire family each held one of the ferrets they used for their job. Richard Dimbleby's one request was 'Please don't ask me to hold them'.

A weekly feature of *Down Your Way* was the interview with a local family. Often we would arrive at someone's home to find the children, freshly washed and dressed in their best, naturally a trifle nervous at the arrival of such a well-known broadcasting personality. Within minutes and with a 'I've got some like you lot at home', Richard would have broken the ice, and there he would be down on the floor playing with trains, aeroplanes, animals, and any other toys which happened to be handy. The larger the family the better he liked it. I cannot remember exactly what the record was, but I know it was in excess of fifteen children in one mammoth interview.

Once we took *Down Your Way* under the sea in H.M. Submarine *Alaric*. Richard, nervous lest he be incapacitated by sea sickness – he was not a good sailor – crammed himself and me too with anti-seasickness pills before entering the submarine. Some of these remedies were based, in those days, on a drug with rather difficult side effects, which blurred the taker's vision for a while. We both experienced some difficulty in negotiating the narrow gang plank leading from the depot ship *Maidstone*, much to the amusement of the submarine crews, who clearly thought 'Here come the BBC, drunk again, and at 8 o'clock in the morning too'.

Richard's sense of fun could often be employed to good advantage in finding original material for the programme. Whilst doing the research work for a programme from Bond Street, London, I thought it might be amusing to have an interview with someone very well known to Richard, but who was seated in the chair of a beauty parlour, and whose face was entirely obscured by a face-pack beauty preparation. I had of course to tell Richard enough about this person, without giving the game away, to enable him to conduct the interview. He readily agreed, but his one worry was that when the well-known person's face was revealed he might not recognise her. However, in the end he accepted my assurances. There was no doubt about his recognition, amidst shouts of surprise and a gale of laughter, of his own wife Dilys. In order to arrange this little bit of fun an enormous amount of cloak and dagger work had to be carried out. Since Richard was such an astute man I feared he would guess the secret well in advance if any hint of what was afoot was allowed to leak out. I had to meet Dilys beforehand in the strictest secrecy, and on the day of recording my wife conducted her to the beauty salon, whilst I kept Richard busy recording at the other end of Bond Street. In fact, he did not even know she was in London on that particular day.

After the war, whilst lunching with Tom Chalmers, then Head of the Light Programme, Richard Dimbleby is reported to have remarked '*Down Your Way* is the world's easiest programme. It's money for jam.' 'Well, if you think that, you can have it', replied Chalmers. Some three years and 150 programmes later Richard had changed his mind. For him the routine went on week after week without a break, involving perhaps an all-night journey by sleeping car to some distant town, a long day's work there, and an all-night journey back again. As with Aberdeen for example – 1,200 miles and a full day's work in thirty-six hours. Alternatively, he might have to journey down from London on a Tuesday evening, record all day Wednesday, and journey back on Thursday simply because there was no other convenient train.

Being an old newspaperman himself, Richard always went out of his way to help the local press, who showed an intense interest in *Down Your Way*. This was particularly so if there was a young or inexperienced reporter present, when Richard would deliberately throw out a gag line at his own expense. Arriving in Bognor Regis dressed in one of his favourite suits of herringbone tweed, a herringbone wool waistcoat, and a tie of obscure tartan, Richard was full of beans. 'Ah, I see they have

featured my arrival' he remarked, drawing attention to a wrestling poster. 'Abdul the terrible Turk – that's me.'

There was the picture which appeared on the front cover of *Radio Times* of Richard Dimbleby riding on the back of a Hereford bull at Wantage. We had just finished recording at a local farm, when a free-lance photographer, who happened to be driving by, asked Dimbleby to pose with the bull. The farmer suggested that he should climb up on its back as it was quite used to that sort of thing. Despite a tight recording schedule Richard obliged, and the photographer went happily away with his scoop.

Another photographer, John McNulty, followed the BBC tour of Wisbech with an enormous reflex camera. At one stop when the party was posed for photographs, Richard commented on the size of the camera. 'You haven't seen half,' said John. 'It plays records too.' 'And I suppose you keep your lunch in a spare corner of it,' Richard retorted.

At the next stop John was missing, but rushed in breathlessly as the party were preparing to move. 'A moment, Mr Dimbleby,' he said, flourishing his camera, 'just one more picture.'

Dimbleby posed again. John hesitated. Something was wrong with the camera. He fiddled with the back – and produced a large paper bag full of sandwiches.

Charles Freer adds this footnote on one of the many occasions when 'Down Your Way' visited Ireland. They had gone to a tourist hotel for a meal at about 8 o'clock in the evening:

Having sat in the dining room for a full twenty minutes, Richard beckoned to a waitress and enquired if we were going to get any service. She disappeared into the kitchens and in about five minutes she came back and said, 'I'm sorry you've been kept waiting, but I'm afraid you'll have to wait a while longer for the Head Waiter's having his dinner.' I remember Richard's reply: 'Well, who am I to interfere with a waiter's meal break. Ask him to leave some dinner for the guests.'

Only once did Dimbleby fail to go Down Your Way. A riding accident forced him to do the programme from his house, by remote control.

In 1953 he handed over the programme to Franklin Engelmann, who has written this:

I ought to tell you that until 1965 listeners still wrote to Richard as the interviewer on *Down Your Way* twelve years after he relinquished it. Of course, a proportion had stopped listening to it at that time and so were unaware of the change, but the rest must have genuinely thought his was the voice of the programme, so great was his impact. Local journalists have said to my face: 'And what time does Mr Dimbleby arrive?'

The letters Richard passed on to me with a wryly amused 'Yours, I think, Jingle' written on the corner.

Down Your Way from home

The 200th edition of Twenty Questions with Jack Train, Joy Adamson and Anona Winn

The 200th edition of Twenty Questions with Jack Train, Joy Adamson and Anona Winn

Richard Dimbleby's other great radio programme was Twenty Questions, a game in which he could use his very quick intelligence to amuse a huge mass audience. He always recognised that broadcasts must be entertaining and he never lost his flair for showmanship. He stayed on Twenty Questions for eighteen years, with Gilbert Harding and then Kenneth Horne as chairmen, and Anona Winn, Joy Adamson and Jack Train as the other regular members of the team. Mike Meehan, for long the producer of Twenty Questions, recalls:

MIKE MEEHAN

Twenty Questions

I remember one evening, while we waited for the programme to start, Jack Train, a past master in story telling, turned to Richard and said, 'I don't know whether I've told you this one before.' 'Is it funny?' asked Richard. 'Yes,' replied Jack. 'Then,' retorted Richard, 'I haven't heard it!'

During one programme, when the chairman was the late Gilbert Harding, Richard sat quietly, while the other members of the team talked over one another in trying to 'find' the object. Gilbert, annoyed by their chatter, called a halt, turned to Richard and said, 'You're very quiet, Richard.' 'Yes,' replied Richard, 'I'm just waiting for the others to wear themselves out.'

Once when we were discussing the different ways the team members played Twenty Questions, Anona Winn confessed to hating 'abstracts' because, she said, 'I have a photographic mind, and like to snatch a clue that flashes a picture of something tangible in my mind's eye.' Later that evening her 'solo' was 'The missing arms of Venus'. She, as usual in her solos, got it eventually. Richard promptly asked, 'Well, what did your mind's eye see then? Venus or her arms?'

And Anona Winn herself adds:

I remember the evening when Richard's 'solo' was 'a weighing machine'. I think he had an idea of this, early in his questioning, but he went on in a mischievous vein with: 'Is it used by men and women?' 'Is it publicly owned as well as privately?' 'Does one pay to use it?' 'How much?'

When the answer to his last question turned out to be 'a penny', Richard sighed an enormous sad sigh and said, 'Ah well, I've enjoyed the years I've had with the BBC.'

It got an enormous laugh from the audience, who had been rocking all through the questioning.

Kenneth Horne writes:

We all had tremendous admiration for him. He was unselfish to a degree, especially in the actual game of *Twenty Questions*. But what impressed me was the fact that he never tried to show anyone up. Many a time I have given an answer which he knew to be wrong, but he thought it a poor show to correct 'The Chairman'.

During the three or four years that we knew he was ill (he told us), he always appeared in the best of spirits, and indeed he *looked* well too.

Never pompous – never.

Norman Hackforth, for many years the 'Mystery Voice' of Twenty Questions, became one of Richard Dimbleby's closest friends, and took his place in the team for the 1965 series. He recalls an incident which had nothing to do with the panel game:

In January 1955 I was in Jamaica, playing an engagement at a hotel on the north shore. My wife was at that moment on the high seas, on a small banana boat on her way to join me.

At 7 o'clock one morning my telephone rang, and a voice asked if I would be ready at eight o'clock to take a call from London from Mr Richard Dimbleby.

I told them I would, and then proceeded to work myself into a fever of anxiety, wondering why on earth Richard should be telephoning me all the way from London. By 7.30 I was firmly convinced that something ghastly had happened to Pamela, and that Richard, my loyal friend, had said: 'Leave it to me. I will break the news to him.' The minutes dragged by and at last, at nearly 8.15, the phone rang again.

'Hackett?' a cheerful and familiar voice enquired, 'this is Dimbleby.' 'Yes, Dick,' I replied. 'What has happened? Where are you?' 'Oh, I'm at London Airport, covering the departure of Princess Margaret to Jamaica, for television. I just thought it would be a good idea to find out from you how the weather is there.'

I looked out of the window, and burst out laughing. 'If you really want to know,' I said, 'it's – *hissing* with rain!' And it was, too!

Just another instance of the master's passion for authentic detail.

Alongside Twenty Questions and Down Your Way Dimbleby was doing more and more work for the expanding television service. He turned his versatile hand to all kinds of broadcasts – commentaries on the Lord Mayor's Show and the Boat Race, 'Other People's Jobs', visits to the Zoo and to many other parts of 'London Town' or places 'About Britain'. Those were the days before either a daily television news service or Panorama.

Dimbleby in Other People's Jobs.

Top: hauled aboard the Southend lifeboat, 1950

Middle: with Sylvia Peters, television announcer, and waitresses in training, 1950

Bottom: serving a BOAC meal to air hostess Barbara Jupp, 'London Town', 1953

Something No One Expected

In the old days of Television Newsreel (which existed between 1948 and 1954 and was entirely on film) Richard Dimbleby used to introduce a Sunday edition called 'Weekly Review'. This consisted of nothing more than excerpts from the week's newsreels interspersed with filmed links that Richard used to record on Friday evenings. The complications of this are hard to believe nowadays. For Union reasons, the film laboratories would only process our film on weekdays, up to and including Friday night, but on two or three occasions a year – by agreement with the cinema newsreels – they were prepared to work on Saturdays if there was a major sporting event. Richard's links for 'Weekly Review' did not qualify under this agreement, so they still had to be done on the Friday night.

So on the eve of the Boat Race, on the Friday night, Richard Dimbleby found himself recording a comment on a race that hadn't yet happened. This worked perfectly well in 1950, so we decided to risk it again in 1951, and I remember that Friday night very well.

We ran the cameras:

'And so,' said Richard, 'Cambridge win the Boat race for the fifty-third time.'

'That's fine,' I said, 'now do the other one.'

The cameras ran again.

'And so,' said Richard, 'Oxford win the Boat Race for the forty-fourth time.'

We were all laughing about this and then Richard said:

'What happens if they tie?'

This seemed most unlikely and we couldn't think of a possible remark which would be suitable. For one thing we didn't know how many ties there had been before. And then, as much for a joke as anything else, we hit on the idea of recording:

'Well, that's something no one expected to happen.'

The next day Oxford sank.

*In June 1950 Richard Dimbleby received a letter from the company
which laid the first telegraphic cable across the English Channel suggesting
television might like to celebrate the forthcoming centenary of the event.
He talked to Peter Dimmock, and a series of technical, municipal and diplomatic negotiations followed. At 9.30 p.m. on 27 August 1950 the television
announcer at Alexandra Palace was able to say:*

On 28 August 1850 the first telegram was sent from England to
France by means of a cable laid across the Straits of Dover. Tonight –
in a very few minutes – television pictures transmitted to Alexandra
Palace from one of our mobile outside broadcast units at this moment
in Calais will not only mark the centenary of that historic achievement
of the last century, but herald in a new and important era in international communication.

*Television had at last crossed the Channel. Richard Dimbleby was there
to show viewers in Britain their first live sight of the floodlit Calais Town
Hall. He was subsequently present on every major occasion when live British
television opened its window wider still and wider on to the world outside.
This time it was Calais en fête, followed three days later by a children's
programme from France. Soon it was to be a whole week of collaboration
with the French Television Service:*

BERKELEY SMITH

Television from France

The first time that we in the BBC worked with the new-found French
Television Service in 1952, in a week of common programmes called 'La
Grande Semaine', found Richard in his element. Not only was his French
remarkably fluent, but he loved France and had a great sympathy for the
French way of life. I remember particularly one of these early programmes, a relay from the Louvre with Richard as the British commentator and myself as co-producer, with a very talented French director
whose experience and reputation in the film world was considerable,
but whose knowledge of the mechanics of television was necessarily
limited. Since a British outside broadcast unit was handling the broadcast, I asked René to show us what he would like covered in the Louvre
and in particular what areas required special lighting.

As the three of us walked from salle to salle, and René's list of priorities
grew larger and larger, it became obvious that he was blissfully ignorant
of the technical restrictions of an outside broadcast unit. When finally
we reached salle number fourteen, I felt obliged to tell René that in terms
of continuous live television there was not enough light generated in
Paris, nor enough camera cable manufactured in my country, to cover
all that he wished to show to British viewers in the Louvre. 'Courage,
mon brave,' cried René and swept us on to the next room. Richard
thought it all a splendid Gallic joke and, as he said, 'That'll teach you to
be a pedestrian British O.B. producer'. And, of course, he was right.
While we in the BBC started that week vaguely contemptuous of the

With Line Renaud and André Claveau

technical ignorance of our French colleagues, I for one finished with a very healthy respect for their imaginative approach to television.

The only time I ever saw Richard lose his temper was in a later programme in that same visit. This was a relay from the Bateau Mouche, one of the river boats on the Seine, and was intended to be a study in French elegance, taste and talent, involving a mannequin show interspersed with top French artists like Jean Sablon, the whole set against the fabulous backdrop of the Paris skyline on a warm July night. It should have been a winner, but for a number of reasons, mainly technical, but in part ones of temperament, this broadcast turned out to be a disaster on such an imperial scale that a long-suffering Cecil McGivern, then the BBC's Controller of Programmes, ordered the programme to be faded halfway through the transmission. All this time Richard as compère had been keeping a brave face as chaos developed backstage. When the cease fire finally went and McGivern withdrew his troops, Richard walked down the gangplank white with anger, throwing, if I remember rightly, a couple of bottles of champagne and a chair into the Seine, saying in a cold hard voice 'I'll never work with these clots again'. Whereupon the unhappy French technicians, who had been primarily

With Sylvia Peters and Etienne Lalou, French commentator

73

responsible for the breakdown, looked up at Richard with admiration, recognising in their terms a man of spirit and élan who for ever afterwards had a special position in the affections of the French Television Service.

In those most difficult of programmes, involving co-operation between two headstrong and highly nationalistic television services, speaking two separate languages, it was always Richard who best survived the heat of the day. When we'd finished, usually very late at night, we would pile into the back of the big open Jaguar he had at that time and in the heady warmth of a July night he would drive down the Champs Elysées with all the verve and skill of a French taxi driver, on our way to what quite often was our first proper meal of the day. But whatever time we might get back to our hotel, Richard never ever made the mistake of leaving undone his homework for the following day. At one or two in the morning we'd be back in his room, checking the details of the next broadcast, as he wrote, in that large rather flowery hand, his notes on cards which he carried with him and used in his commentaries all over the world.

Dimbleby became the principal BBC commentator at State occasions both for radio and for television. His choice of words, his measured delivery, were never more attuned with the feelings of his listeners than when he described the Lying-in-State of King George VI to a sorrowing nation:

RICHARD DIMBLEBY

Westminster Hall, 12 February 1952

It is dark in New Palace Yard at Westminster tonight. As I look down from this old, leaded window I can see the ancient courtyard dappled with little pools of light where the lamps of London try to pierce the biting, wintry gloom and fail. And moving through the darkness of the night is an even darker stream of human beings, coming, almost noiselessly, from under a long, white canopy that crosses the pavement and ends at the great doors of Westminster Hall. They speak very little, these people, but their footsteps sound faintly as they cross the yard and go out through the gates, back into the night from which they came.

They are passing, in their thousands, through the hall of history while history is being made. No one knows from where they come or where they go, but they are the people, and to watch them pass is to see the nation pass.

It is very simple, this Lying-in-State of a dead King, and of incomparable beauty. High above all light and shadow and rich in carving is the massive roof of chestnut, that Richard II put over the great Hall. From that roof the light slants down in clear, straight beams, unclouded by any dust, and gathers in a pool at one place. There lies the coffin of the King.

The oak of Sandringham, hidden beneath the rich golden folds of the Standard; the slow flicker of the candles touches gently the gems of the Imperial Crown, even that ruby that King Henry wore at Agincourt. It touches the deep purple of the velvet cushion and the cool, white flowers of the only wreath that lies upon the flag. How moving can such simplicity be. How real the tears of those who pass and see it, and come out again, as they do at this moment in unbroken stream, to the cold, dark night and a little privacy for their thoughts.

Who can know what they are thinking? Does that blind man whom they lead so carefully down the thick carpet sense around him the presence of history? Does he know that Kings and Queens have feasted here and stood their trial and gone to their death? And that little woman, with the airman by her side – does she feel the ghosts that must be here in the shadows of the Hall? The men and the women of those tumultuous days of long ago, of Chaucer, Essex, Anne Boleyn, Charles and Cromwell, Warren Hastings and those early Georges? Or does she, and do all those over seventy thousand of the nation, who will have passed through this day alone, think only of the sixth George; the faithful George who lies there now, guarded by the living statues of his officers and Gentlemen at Arms and Yeomen of the Guard. For in the few seconds that are all that can be given to each subject to pass by his dead King, there is colour and splendour and loveliness beyond compare.

I thought when I watched the Bearers take the coffin into this Hall yesterday that I had never seen a sight so touching. The clasped arms of the Grenadiers, the reverent care with which they lifted and carried their King. But I was wrong. For in the silent tableau of this Lying-in-State there is a beauty that no movement can ever bring. He would be forgiven who believed that these Yeomen of the Bodyguard, facing outwards from the corners of the catafalque, were carven statues of the Yeomen of the Tudor Henry's day. Could any living man, let alone a white-bearded man of eighty, be frozen into this immobility? The faces of the two Gentlemen at Arms are hidden by the long, white helmet plumes that have fallen about them like a curtain as they bowed their heads. Are they real, those faces, or do the plumes conceal two images of stone? And the slim, straight figures of the officers of the Household Brigade, hands poised lightly on their arms reversed, what sense of pride and honour holds their swords so still that not one gleam of light shall be reflected from a trembling blade? Never safer, better guarded lay a sleeping King than this, with a golden light to warm his resting place and the muffled tread of his devoted people to keep him company. They come from a mile away in the night, moving pace by pace in hours of waiting, come into the silent majesty of the scene and as silently leave again.

Two hundred thousand may come to Westminster this week, but for every one of them there will be a thousand scattered about the world who cannot come, but who may be here in their thoughts at this moment. They will know that the sorrow of one man, one woman or one child that passes by the King in London is their sorrow too.

For how true tonight of George the Faithful is that single sentence spoken by an unknown man of his beloved father: 'The sunset of his death tinged the whole world's sky.'

Sir Anthony Wagner, who succeeded Sir George Bellew in the post of Garter King of Arms, understood well how Dimbleby prepared his commentaries for the great State occasions. He described these preparations in 'The Times':

GARTER KING OF ARMS

The Gratitude of Posterity

A principal claim of Richard Dimbleby on the gratitude of his contemporaries and of posterity is that he originated and established the new profession and art of commentator on the great occasions and Ceremonies of State. This he did with such authority and mastery that, for those who witnessed these performances and the preparations for them, the final question in future will always be 'Was this as Dimbleby would have done it?'

Those who merely saw the finished product, with its utter ease and smoothness, would not easily understand the effort and difficulty of the preparation. The sheer physical complexity of the movements has first to be grasped. Different people start from widely separated places at slightly different times, so exactly timed that each will arrive at the

Opposite: Lying-in-State, King George VI

76

precisely right moment at his exact place in the order of proceeding. Dimbleby had first to learn who they all were, where they were coming from, where they were going to and why. He then had to plan his commentary, switching from one to another, in such a way as to do justice to all, but especially to the main theme: to make clear and simple to his audience a complex pattern of many threads; and to keep that audience interested through the sometimes lengthy preparatory stages as well as the main performance.

Over and above all this he had to expand and do full justice to the additional dimension of history. These occasions are what they are because they and their special form have been wrought and hammered out by the long, unbroken process of our history. The audience must be given the essence of this background, but not bored with too much of it.

In all these aspects, Dimbleby was supreme. His preparations were immensely thorough. He came before rehearsals and to rehearsals, studied papers, asked questions, and was content with nothing less than a complete grasp of what would happen and why. And in his final performance the clear exposition of complexity, the vivid and sometimes humorous description, and the solemnity and sense of history were blended in just the right proportions.

It was at the Queen's Coronation in 1953 that he first established his authority in these matters. Only after much searching of heart had it been agreed that so intimate and sacred a ceremony could be shown on television. I remember the doubts beforehand and the feeling after Dimbleby's triumphant performance that here was something that could be done not merely without offence or loss but with great advantage.

Dimbleby published his own account of his experiences in Westminster Abbey in the 'Sunday Dispatch' five days after the Queen's Coronation on 2 June 1953:

RICHARD DIMBLEBY

My Coronation Commentary

In all my experience of State ceremonies – and I have described most of them in the past ten or fifteen years for the BBC – I have never known one go so quickly. I think that this was due to the wonderful colour of the scene in the Abbey and because it was changing all the time. There was always something to watch.

I left my yacht, the *Vabel*, on the river in a police launch at a quarter past five on Coronation morning, and I was in my box in the triforium of the Abbey at 5.30. I sat in the box without a break until 2.30 in the afternoon – nine hours. But it felt like no more than two or three. All my colleagues of the BBC had the same experience. It was almost impossible to believe that virtually a whole working day had passed since we came in.

The commentators' box that had been built by the Ministry of Works for the BBC was a miniature house occupying the two central arches of

the triforium, or upper gallery of the Abbey, and in the middle of the eastern end . . . in other words, immediately behind the High Altar.

This 'house', which was so completely sound-proofed that it would have been possible to shout at the top of one's voice inside it without being heard by somebody standing outside the door, was divided into four rooms.

John Snagge and Howard Marshall, who were the commentators for sound radio, occupied the ground floor left, while the ground floor right was filled by a television cameraman and his camera, of necessity so cramped that he was only just able to sit upright.

On the upper floor the room on the left was occupied by two French commentators, one talking to France for sound radio and television combined (a Herculean task) and the other to French-speaking Canada for radio.

The whole of the 'coverage' of the historic ceremony as far as television and sound at home and abroad were concerned came from this minute 'house', which was connected with the sound control room in the Dean's Verger's room and with the television control in a hut built just outside the Abbey.

The existence of the commentators during the day was reasonably comfortable though rather cramped. Certainly we had an unrivalled view of the whole proceedings, thanks largely to the personal interest taken by the Earl Marshal, the Duke of Norfolk, who climbed up to the triforium one day, a few weeks in advance of The Day, to survey the site and decide on the spot what accommodation should be provided.

One of my outstanding memories of the whole Coronation was, indeed, the kindness of the Earl Marshal. Anyone who believes that this peer, with a castle and big sporting interests, had a sinecure in his – if I may use the expression – stage management of the occasion is utterly mistaken.

Here was a man who carried the entire burden of the arrangements on his own shoulders, who knew every detail, and personally worked out every timetable. I do not think that he could have had more than a few hours' rest at any time during the eight months preceding this week.

Nevertheless he found time to attend meetings with the BBC and the newsreel organisations to discuss technical details, to go to Broadcasting House to listen to recordings made at the previous Coronation in 1937, to invite the three BBC commentators to luncheon privately so that we could talk over any problems, and to attend the BBC television studios at Lime Grove on the Saturday before the Coronation so that any such minute difficulties could be resolved.

He is also a man of quite tremendous humour. He told me that, having observed some of the staff officers fidgeting during the final rehearsal in the Abbey, he sent them a message ordering them to stop and reminding them that 'there is plenty of room in the Tower'.

The same could be said of that jolly, entirely natural and charming man, the Archbishop of Canterbury, who has the knack of putting one completely at ease. He confounded me by saying when we met in the Abbey at a rehearsal two weeks ago: 'What wonderful progress your pigs are making.'

For the moment I thought I had misunderstood his remark until he explained that he had been staying with one of his sons who lives in our village and had seen my piggery and the latest litter. Thereafter each conversation we had in the Abbey was always prefaced by a remark or two about the pigs, to the astonishment of the sundry Officers of State who were standing near.

I cannot deny that I found my task of acting as television commentator for the Abbey ceremony an exacting one, but it was an honour of which I am very proud. The essence of the whole thing is that timing should be precise. The duty of any television commentator is to say just enough and no more, although there are times when the effect of what is being shown on the screen is infinitely greater if it takes place in silence.

Thus, in the Abbey there were moments in the ceremony which had to be left uncovered by speech but which were preceded immediately by ritual which needed explanation. It was, therefore, vital to know extactly how long this ritual took and to prepare a note or 'rubric' which fitted that time precisely.

This, I think, was the greatest strain, to speak at a critical moment, knowing that within a second or two something must happen over which one must not speak, or even that Her Majesty or the Archbishop were about to speak.

So thorough had been the rehearsals that we were able to fit this jig-saw together successfully, being caught only once, when the Archbishop proceeded directly to a prayer when at rehearsals he had paused before uttering it. Such details in retrospect may seem very trivial, but it is close attention to them that gives any great occasion its maximum effect.

Details, of course, are what one remembers most when looking back on the occasion. I remember when the Duke of Cornwall first appeared by the side of his grandmother, the Queen Mother, in the Royal Box. We had been waiting for this, of course, and for an awful moment I thought that he was in a position in which our cameras could not see him.

His presence in the Abbey for the Coronation of his mother had been so widely publicised beforehand that we never would have been forgiven for not showing him to the millions of those looking in on television. You may imagine my relief when I heard the voice of Peter Dimmock, the television producer at the Abbey, saying in my headphones: 'I have got a lovely shot of Charles – mention him as soon as you like.'

Then there was the charming paternal attitude of the Bishop of Durham [now Archbishop of Canterbury], who by ancient tradition stands on the right hand of the Sovereign during the whole ceremony. I am sure that millions of people watching their television screens must have seen the continuous glances which he gave the Queen, almost as though he were saying: 'Don't worry, my dear . . . it is going beautifully.'

It reminded me exactly of a father nursing his daughter through some trying ordeal, though in fact the Queen needed no encouragement at all. She had attended several rehearsals, taking part in them herself, and quite obviously knew the whole ceremony.

Though her attitude throughout was devout, indeed humble, since this was largely a Communion service in which she was partaking, I saw

her at the moment when the Mistress of the Robes was adjusting the gown of white linen that she wore for the anointing give an almost imperceptible signal with her right hand behind her back that enough adjustment had been made and that she was now to be left alone.

Another moment in the service I found very touching was the homage paid to his wife by the Duke of Edinburgh. The historic form of service laid down for the Coronation demands that the Princes of the Blood and the Peers when kneeling before the Sovereign shall first give their Christian name and title.

For example, the Duke of Norfolk said: 'I, Bernard, Duke of Norfolk...'. I wonder how many people noticed that the Duke of Edinburgh only gave his Christian name and omitted any title? Was it perhaps because he wanted the Queen to know that he was paying homage to her as her husband and not simply as one of the Royal Princes?

I must also mention the splendid bearing and dignity of Sir George Bellew, who as Garter King of Arms was responsible for a great deal of the detailed 'stage management' on the floor of the Coronation theatre. 'Garter', as he is known, is a living encyclopaedia on all matters appertaining to State affairs. I have never known him at a loss to answer immediately and correctly the most difficult technical question. Signals which he gave in his capacity as King of Arms during the ceremony for various movements were a model of efficiency and unobtrusiveness.

One little thing slightly marred the glorious memories. When I was in the Abbey in the evening while we were preparing the television epilogue which we put on the air unannounced at 11.30 I saw the melancholy sight of the litter left behind by the peers.

It seemed to me amazing that even on this occasion we could not break ourselves of one of our worst national habits. Tiers and tiers of stalls on which the peers had been sitting were covered with sandwich wrappings, sandwiches, morning newspapers, fruit peel, sweets and even a few empty miniature bottles. Let us be fair however, and remember that the peers, many of them elderly men, had sat in their places, some of them seeing very little of the ceremony, for seven hours.

Perhaps it was because the day was so cold that no casualties at all were reported to the ambulance teams hidden away within the Abbey. One herald fainted during the final rehearsal and one page was taken ill. During the actual ceremony no human failing marred the proceedings, in sharp contrast to the considerable casualty list at the Coronation of King George VI in 1937.

During Tuesday's ceremony I heard an American say: 'This is the only country in the world that could stage such a wonderful show.'

His choice of words could be improved upon, perhaps, but his meaning was quite clear. It was a very moving experience, even for one as urgently preoccupied as I was with the details of the occasion, to see a ceremony being performed which would be recorded in the children's history books 500 years hence.

I felt profoundly conscious that I was seeing history in the making, and, indeed, the whole pageant on the floor of the Abbey moved with a slow irresistible rhythm that seemed to lift it out of time altogether.

I thought at one moment as I half-closed my eyes and watched the measured ceremony being carried through that I might be watching something that had happened a thousand years before. In all that time there has been no major change in our Coronations: the lovely robes of the great officers of State, the gleaming swords, the Crown Jewels, the massed assembly of bishops in scarlet and white, and the matchless setting of the Abbey itself – belonging not to one year or to one century but to our history.

This curiously detached emotion was not just the hypnotic effect of a great occasion. During the past two days I have been working with Brian George, who is in command of all recording operations at the BBC, making a permanent gramophone recording of the great occasion.

This has necessitated playing over several times recordings of last Tuesday's ceremony.

It is an extraordinary thing that the thrill of emotion that I felt when I heard the lovely music and singing and the beautiful spoken words of the Archbishop during the actual ceremony has returned every time that the recordings were played. There is, indeed, a strange quality about the Coronation ceremony. It makes it quite different from any other great occasion in our national life.

There were moments during the ceremony when my emotion must have been obvious to listeners. For example, when I saw the Queen's Champion so proudly bearing the Queen's Standard in the procession, a man whose family has defended the honour of their Sovereign without a break since days of William the Conqueror, I found it very difficult to control my voice and speak properly at all.

John Snagge, in the adjoining box, told me that he felt precisely the same emotion.

I believe that we as a nation have done ourselves a profound service by showing to the world how unchanging are the traditions and pride which are our foundations. Visitors from abroad who were in London on Tuesday were envious of everything they saw, and none more so than the Americans – a race of such vitality but so lacking in tradition – who know that they must wait a thousand years before they can show the world anything so significant or so lovely.

I have never been so tired as I was when I finally left the Abbey at half-past midnight on Tuesday – seventeen hours after I entered it. I have never felt so acutely the strain of describing a great public occasion, and I have never before had such a feeling of nervousness and anxiety before the day began.

But I have never been so proud or so glad that I was able to contribute in a small way to history, even to making a fragment of history, because this was the first time that the Coronation of a British Sovereign had ever been seen as it happened except by the privileged few in the Abbey.

D. R. G. MONTAGUE

Under Escort

Rehearsing the Coronation broadcast

I had a position high up in the triforium from which my camera lenses protruded just sufficiently for operational coverage, but not so intrusively as to be noticeable or distracting. I had to buy a grey shirt to match the colour of the surrounding stonework to complete the camouflage.

Every detail had to be considered and the most meticulous arrangements applied to every facet of this, the most important television broadcast yet undertaken. Behind the triforium, the Ministry of Works had set up a network of hastily constructed rooms or cubicles for operational requirements. I was in one of these – rather like a wooden cell, with the roof too low for me to stand up straight, but equipped with a box seat and an electric fan.

I used to enter with a sort of Groucho Marx straddle and make for the box seat where I could straighten up sitting down – a paradox this, but comfortably true. From this seat I evolved numerous permutations of kneeling and sitting positions from which to make necessary adjustments and operational manoeuvres to the camera. My sole contact with the outside world once the door was shut was through my camera microphone and headphones – a sort of umbilical cord keeping me in contact with the busy, beating heart of the television control room in some other claustrophobic corner of the Abbey.

In the cubicle over mine was Richard Dimbleby. He seemed to have more room than I, for I could often hear him striding his floor above my head. I envied him his head room. We knew each other very well by this time through many previous programmes. He always used to call me 'Monty' and this name has stuck ever since.

In the early days of Euro-vision viewers in France, the Netherlands, Belgium and Western Germany saw the Coronation live with their own commentators following Dimbleby's words

With the numerous rehearsals and tests which had to be carried out during the week prior to the Coronation, we were often unable to leave our positions for hours at a time. The cubicles opened out on to a main corridor which was virtually a gallery around that section of the Abbey, part of which led to an enclosure with seats for peers and their ladies.

An essential facility on this floor were some toilets which had been erected specially for the occasion and separately and suitably inscribed 'PEERS' and 'PEERESSES'. For the purposes of this occasion, Richard and I were temporarily ennobled, as it were. But visiting the 'PEERS' was no ordinary matter. One could not just nip smartly away and come back at leisure. There were very strict security precautions and arrangements.

You had to wait outside the door of your own cubicle, and in good time (if you were lucky and traffic was light) a uniformed official would arrive to escort you there and back. I shall always remember Richard waiting with patience and apprehension outside his cubicle, trying to catch the eye of this uniformed flunkey, just as one would hail a bus, and proceeding under escort to the 'PEERS' and eventually back again. This solemn ritual was carried out with all the dignity worthy of the occasion.

LEONARD MIALL

How America saw the Coronation

Dimbleby thought, and it made him angry, that the relay of his Coronation commentary from the Abbey had been interrupted on one American television magazine programme by a facetious interview with a resident chimpanzee called J. Fred Muggs.

I was the BBC's chief correspondent in America at the time, and saw the offending programme. It was in fact the live radio commentaries of Howard Marshall and John Snagge that were interrupted, when shortwave reception faltered, for this graceless enterprise. Richard Dimbleby, on the contrary, suddenly achieved transatlantic fame and respect.

The rival American television networks were hotly competing for the best and fastest coverage of the Coronation. The first to get pictures on to the American air would scoop a huge expectant audience. This was, of course, before the development of videotape recording or live transatlantic transmission by satellite.

As soon as the Coronation date was announced the Earl Marshal was asked to estimate at what exact time the Archbishop could be expected to lower the crown on to the Queen's head. (His forecast, made months ahead, was correct to within one minute.) The American networks made elaborate and secretive arrangements to send their own ace commentators to London and to rush the films and telerecordings up to the moment of crowning back to the United States as fast as possible.

Ed Murrow, then in charge of news for the Columbia Broadcasting System, chartered a Stratocruiser from BOAC, ripped out the seats, installed film processing and editing machines, and arranged to work in this flying laboratory and cutting room so that the film, with his own commentary, would be ready for immediate transmission.

The National Broadcasting Company made similar preparations with another airline and also arranged with the Venezuelan Air Force that on 2 June it would conveniently take delivery of a much faster Canberra bomber ordered from Britain. Of course it would have to stop in America on the way, and could drop off cans of film exclusively for NBC. (In the event that Canberra developed engine trouble after two hours and had to turn back.)

The American Broadcasting Company was at that time a poor third in the television stakes, and could not afford such outlays. It settled for booking a coaxial cable to the nearest point in Canada to pick up whatever the Canadian Broadcasting Corporation showed.

In fact the transatlantic race was won by an RAF Canberra which brought the BBC telerecording to Canada. Thus it was Richard Dimbleby's Abbey Commentary, relayed by ABC-TV, to which avid United States viewers first switched. The American republic suddenly realised that Britain could not only stage glorious coronations. She also had outstanding television production skill, and an exceptional television commentator.

The week after the Coronation BBC television cameras were present at the Royal School of Needlework Exhibition at St James's Palace, which the Queen Mother was to visit. Dimbleby began his commentary five minutes before Her Majesty was due to arrive, but, unexpectedly for Royalty, she was late and he had to speak for a further twenty minutes during which he treated viewers to a detailed history of the Royal School. It transpired subsequently that the Queen Mother was watching the programme at Clarence House when it started, and was so enthralled that she left her home rather later than she had planned.

Soon after she arrived at nearby St James's Palace she saw Dimbleby and made straight for him with a word of greeting and congratulation on his Coronation commentary. The stick microphone in Dimbleby's hand was live, and viewers heard her say, 'Good evening. . .'. Quick-thinking as he bowed to the Queen Mother, Dimbleby held the microphone under the tails of his evening dress to muffle the sound and prevent her private conversation and personal congratulations to him from going out over the air.

JEAN METCALFE

Confidence in Ourselves

In Coronation year I was unexpectedly plunged into the deep sea of ceremonial commentating. Distressingly inexperienced, it was hard work keeping my head above water in the company of some of the best commentators in the world. Most difficult of all was my assignment to cover the Royal visit to Northern Ireland, because this involved going ahead on my own to Belfast to set the scene before Richard came over in time for the Queen's arrival.

Everyone was overwhelmingly kind and hospitable, but I felt like someone in the back row of an orchestra which, through some awful circumstance, lacked a conductor. Everyone treated me like a seasoned professional. I tried to behave like one. But inside I felt hopelessly incompetent.

And then Richard arrived. He came to dinner at my host's house. He greeted me not only as a friend but as an equal, a professional colleague. In a matter of minutes his humour – smiling at the touchiness of local politics which had frightened me into silence – and his enthusiasm had cut my inflated nightmares down to size. It was as though the orchestra had a conductor again.

His presence brought everyone working with him a feeling of warm security because of the confidence we had in him. But more than that, and most unselfishly of all, he gave us confidence in ourselves.

Television Centre, 1961

A Man without Jealousy

It was in the Blue Room at Bomber Command Officers' Mess in 1943 that I first met Richard, very briefly. He was sitting alone waiting to lunch with one of our senior staff officers. One of my colleagues approached him and asked if he would care for a drink. 'I don't usually drink at lunchtime, but you are so kind, I will, thank you.'

Eight years later when I was working at the British Forces Network in Germany in Hamburg he came with the other members of the *Twenty Questions* team. We met again this time at the Garrison Theatre. 'Hullo,' he said, 'I met you some years ago at Bomber Command Headquarters, didn't I? What are you doing getting mixed up in the broadcasting business?'

I had always remembered the first meeting, but there was no reason at all for him to, except that he remembered almost everyone he met no matter how unimportant they were. Ask anyone with whom he worked, from the doorman to the cameraman, and they will tell you the same. They will also recall his immense good humour. One night on *Panorama* he was caught by the camera when he was combing his hair. In the next

With George Cansdale and Dumbo, 1949

evening's *Tonight* we gently ribbed him about it. On his way the following week to the *Panorama* studio he smiled at me and said: 'Tonight, my boy, I'm doing a strip-tease. Follow that if you dare!'

One of the nicest things about Richard was that he was a great source of advice. There was never any sense of jealousy at the threat of challenge of the new boys; instead there was that constant stream of encouragement and, when asked for, help. In 1949, when I was fresh to the television world, he advised me to 'do as much as you can, spread your net wide, go anywhere in order to get experience, any experience in writing, interviewing, producing, directing or commentating. Don't specialise too early, otherwise you will find that you have put yourself in a limited position. The time to start saying no to certain kinds of jobs is later rather than sooner. Once you are in that position always take holidays, never feel yourself getting stale and remember there is more in life than just television. Sometimes I think that we are so concerned with television itself that we forget that we ought to be living and enjoying life just like other people.'

Wise words to a new boy and very welcome words. There were very few in those early days willing to let you take any share in their experience and none was more experienced than Richard. That he cared was a great encouragement.

Dimbleby's advice to get wide experience grew out of his own early training in the complexities of performing in front of the television cameras in a series of programmes produced by Stephen McCormack and written by Peter Hunt:

PETER HUNT

London Town ... About Britain ... About Europe

I first met Richard in 1951. We were both going to the Festival of Britain, I for the BBC's *Picture Page*, he for another television programme. I had lost my BBC staff pass. Richard said, 'Find some piece of paper and wave it about'. I happened to have been working on papers about the Great Exhibition of 1851 and had in my pocket an entry pass to that exhibition of a century before. Following Richard's advice I shoved it in my wallet and used it for several days to enter the Festival with no one noticing.

Shortly afterwards, Stephen McCormack enlisted me to join George Moresby White as co-writer of *London Town*, already a top rating 45-minute television magazine about the world's greatest city.

The mercurial McCormack, loyalist, royalist, empiricist, humorist, was the ideal mentor, foil and friend for the incredibly busy Dimbleby, who was juggling his diary with *Down Your Way*, *Twenty Questions* and much more.

London Town was, in the best of all possible senses, the product of a team – Richard Dimbleby himself, a producer studio director, a film director, two writers, and a production secretary. Looking back, and when I consider how technically difficult it was (at the time), it now

amazes me how much one has to pay these days for sledge-hammers to crack peanuts. Richard earned peanuts for what he did, and so, in fact, did we. No matter: it was tremendous fun. Richard always treated us as professionals, and so did Stephen McCormack, and in this way we learned our trade.

The areas we covered together were enormous. I imagine some people remember *London Town*, with its four or five items, covering such diversities as Lloyd's, the College of Arms, the sewers, the dustmen, Greenwich and Of Alley (that oddly named street called after the Duke *of* Buckingham), Smithfield and Billingsgate, St Bride's and the Tower of London. The brief was to produce a programme about London which would interest the London audience. There was no great social content. We didn't knock anyone; we merely tried to find out how they ticked.

In time, and as BBC television network away from London expanded, *London Town* became *About Britain*.

Stephen Hearst joined me as co-writer for Richard and we went through the team process all over the country. Later we wrote for him in Malta and Vienna before the team broke up.

The machinery was this. McCormack would come with us on reconnaissance to a given area – Wales, Skye, Edinburgh, Cornwall, Ulster. In co-operation with the BBC Sound experts we would construct a script. This started as a film shooting-script, which was handed over to John Rhodes. Whilst Rhodes was filming McCormack and Dimbleby on the spot, Hearst and I would be working up the studio sequences. The machinery was such that filmed shots could be matched with studio sets on back projection.

When it came to the 'live' show much, and indeed all, depended on the professional rapport between Richard and Stephen McCormack. The show was usually studio-based, which meant that Richard had to rehearse and master his exact cues into film, and his moves left to right, right to left. He was dealing on the studio floor with participants who had no experience of marks and moves and telecine. Together with McCormack, he had the knack of putting people at their ease. Hearst and I often wrote the most complicated moves and cuts for him, from film to studio, from set to set across the studio. So far as I can recall he never got one wrong.

Hearst and I were usually up in the production gallery for transmission, standing behind McCormack. He took our badgering with the humour and calm which characterises him. I remember one time when an essential camera failed, McCormack simply said 'good' and pressed on. On the studio floor Dimbleby got the message and reacted as if nothing had happened.

He never queried anything we wrote for him unless it didn't square with his particular view of the world. He would reject anything he thought snide or sour in the commentaries which we used to write for him overnight and sometimes only just before he recorded. I once suggested that he should say that a particular place in Wales was 'ugly'. This he couldn't take and asked for my co-operation in saying that 'X is not the prettiest town I have seen'. A professional without malice is a rare bird.

In 1955 Independent Television started, and both Stephen McCormack and Peter Hunt went off to join its ranks. Richard Dimbleby received many tempting offers from the commercial companies to go over to them: he always refused, never asking the BBC even for a guarantee contract. He was a freelance who wished to broadcast only for the BBC, for fees which were agreed and regularly revised without acrimony.

He was naturally used for all the great state outside broadcasts, but one of his reasons for deciding to stay on the BBC side of the fence (apart from a profound belief in public service broadcasting) was his personal satisfaction that he had at last achieved a weekly current affairs programme in which his past experience in news and his wide knowledge of other countries could be regularly used to proper effect.

93

When I returned from Washington to take over charge of the Television Talks Department at the beginning of 1954 I was intent on developing television journalism. My department had some lively young producers, one of whom was Michael Peacock:

MICHAEL PEACOCK

The Move to Panorama

Panorama from Bristol with Michael Peacock, 31 October 1960

It all began, for me at least, in May 1954. At that time I was 24 and had had only eighteen months' experience of television. Richard Dimbleby was no more than a name to me. I admired his work, but had never met him. He worked on Outside Broadcasts and on *About Britain*, produced by the Documentary Department. I worked in Television Talks Department, which until then had never used Richard. Our paths had never crossed.

The Queen's World Tour was due to finish on 15 May of that year. One afternoon ten days before, Cecil McGivern, our Controller of Television Programmes, was summoned from his Lime Grove office to Broadcasting House. A meeting had been called to co-ordinate radio and television plans for covering the Queen's return to London. One by one the Outside Broadcasts for each stage of the Queen's arrival were noted and checked. Richard Dimbleby, who was reporting the Mediterranean part of the tour for radio, would leave *Britannia* at Gibraltar and fly ahead to London, arriving the day before. He would then give the television commentary for what would be a great State occasion which our cameras would cover throughout from *Britannia*'s arrival in the Pool of London to the Queen's drive home to Buckingham Palace.

To Cecil's surprise the meeting went on to consider the programmes arranged for the evening of 15 May in which the full story of this historic Royal Tour would be told. Those were days of a certain rivalry and jockeying for position between radio and television. The Television Service had in fact no plans for any programme beyond the Outside Broadcast of the Queen's drive through London. Cecil McGivern heard the scale of radio's plans for recapitulating the Queen's journey. Undaunted he calmly announced that the Television Service would also be mounting an evening programme to celebrate the Queen's return and asked how many of the BBC's News Correspondents who had reported the tour could be made available.

The meeting was soon over, and Cecil leapt to a telephone. It was a *Radio Times* Press Day, but the page for 15 May was held in the nick of time. At about 5 p.m. that day I was summoned to Cecil's office. With him I found Grace Wyndham Goldie, my immediate boss, and Joanna Spicer, his programme planner. The situation was explained to me. I was to produce 'Postcript to the Journey', as the programme had been christened, at 7.55 p.m. on 15 May. It would last forty minutes. The Archbishop of Canterbury had agreed to take part. Godfrey Talbot, Audrey Russell and Wynford Vaughan-Thomas would be available. Richard Dimbleby had agreed to be the anchorman. Television Newsreel had undertaken to provide film of the Queen's tour, and there was the possibility of the Commonwealth High Commissioners in London each contributing a message for the programme. 'This is a very important programme for the Television Service', said Cecil meaningfully. I had my marching orders!

For me there followed nine days of gruelling and hectic work, at the end of which I had concocted a very complicated and elaborate programme involving live radio circuits to most of the countries visited by the Queen, a dozen or more film sequences which would have to be commentated 'live', reports from News correspondents who had little or no experience of television, the Archbishop and the High Commissioners, and edited telerecordings of the Outside Broadcasts earlier in the day.

The afternoon of the day before, the script was finished, and at 5 o'clock Richard Dimbleby, just back from Gibraltar, climbed for the first time the narrow stairs up to my office in what had been an attic bedroom in one of the houses adjoining the Lime Grove Studios. He was to climb those stairs countless times during the next ten years, for the *Panorama* office is there to this day.

He came into the room a little warily, his smile taking in the faces he didn't know. We shook hands self-consciously, and after some small talk I gave him a copy of the script. He laughed at its weight and settled down to go through it with me. As the scope and complexity of the programme became apparent to him, he looked at me quizzically. 'You've got yourself a handful here', he said, obviously wondering whether this young man whom he had never met before was going to land him in a technical shambles the following evening.

For the next two hours we went through every detail of the programme. This was my first experience of Richard at work, and it was an eye-opener. Even now, I remember the quickness with which he took my points, and his uncanny ability to see where things might go wrong, and the painstaking way with which he noted down what he had to do or might have to do. At the end of our session his script was covered with notes, and he knew everything there was to know about the programme. I was exhausted, and perhaps he sensed this; for as he stood up to leave, he put his arm on my shoulder and grinned cheerfully. 'Don't worry,' he said, 'it will work all right on the night – provided we hit those telecine cues.' 'It should be a very good programme,' he added kindly. 'See you at about 5 o'clock tomorrow'. And off he went.

In the event, it was a very good programme – thanks to Richard. When radio circuits failed he switched faultlessly into the standby routines worked out the night before. He produced immaculate unscripted commentaries to the edited telerecordings he had not seen before. He hit cue after cue as he promised he would, and kept his head when a large and very heavy camera dolly ran over the foot of the unfortunate studio manager during an unrehearsed tracking shot at the end of the programme (the studio manager was an unsung hero – he didn't even cry out despite a broken bone!).

After this programme it was inevitable that we should ask Richard to be anchorman for the 1955 General Election Results Programme. Then, he showed us all not only his unique skill, but also his extraordinary stamina. Despite a gruelling day of rehearsals while people were voting, he worked in front of the cameras until dawn. He had a couple of hours off to catch a moment of sleep, then opened the programme again well before breakfast with the words, 'Short night, wasn't it', kept going non-stop throughout the following day, and then finished off his two-day stint with the big round-up programme on the Friday evening, which included a well-deserved bouquet from his old friend and wartime colleague Ed Murrow.

General Election 1959

Richard Dimbleby's election marathons were to become world famous. The secret of his extraordinary command of the situation during these very complicated and exacting programmes lay in the card index of information about each constituency which was prepared for him beforehand. In 1959 the preparation of this index went badly wrong. On the Tuesday before Election Thursday it was not finished, and those cards which *had* been prepared were incorrect. Richard took off his coat and lived with the index from then on, going through each constituency card with Stanley Hyland who was drafted in to help. Together they worked right through the Wednesday night. So in 1959 he had no sleep the night before he began his marathon. An extraordinary man!

His last General Election marathon was in October 1964, by which time he had been suffering from cancer for four and a half years. And yet he would not even listen to a hint that he might have a rest in the early hours of the Friday morning. Not a bit of it! And never had I seen him more at ease, more on top of his job, more the life and soul of the programme than during the 1964 Election Results which began with an unexpected curtain raiser in the form of Khrushchev's fall from power. Do you remember George Brown crossing swords with Robin Day in a memorable interview on the Friday afternoon when the tension was almost intolerable and tempers were getting frayed? 'And a Merry Christmas to all our readers!' said Richard as cameras switched back to him. The tension dropped and the programme rolled on.

It was after the 1955 Election Results programme that the idea of a weekly *Panorama* with Richard Dimbleby as anchorman was born. In September 1955, because of the illness of my co-producer, I found myself in sole charge of what was to become the BBC's most important regular programme. With Richard Dimbleby and with Malcolm Muggeridge, Woodrow Wyatt, Max Robertson and, six months later, with Chris Chataway, we set out to explore the virgin lands of weekly television journalism.

For Richard, the years of preparation were over. At last he had a weekly major current affairs programme of his own. At last his skills as a newsman, reporter, commentator, and television professional could come together and find expression in one programme.

I worked with Richard on *Panorama* for four years in all. Memory can be deceptive, but for me *Panorama's* finest hour will always be the autumn of 1956. It was during those dark weeks of the Hungarian revolution and the Suez invasion that *Panorama* grew up. The programme with Richard became a national institution. Thinking back now, my memories of *Panorama* during that troubled time are blurred and confused. Nasser,

Right: Robin Day

the Suez Canal, Budapest, Refugees, Cyprus, Eden, Eisenhower and Stevenson, Khrushchev, the Gaza Strip, Port Said, the United Nations . . . our cameras rolled, our voices strained, our typewriters tore into paper, as each Monday Richard Dimbleby reported the continuing crisis in *Panorama*.

Inevitably, Richard wanted to report these great events at first hand. But an anchorman is an anchorman, and we needed him in the *Panorama* studio. However, he did get to Vienna during this period to report the plight of the thousands of Hungarian refugees who were pouring into the city. As fate would have it, we could not get our Eurovision pictures through from Vienna that Monday night, and for the first time Richard couldn't introduce *Panorama*. Cliff Michelmore, who happened to be in the building, took his place. Half an hour later we had used up all our standby material, and Malcolm Muggeridge and some experts on Russia in the Lime Grove Studio were clearly reaching the end of what they could find to say about Khrushchev. It looked as if we might have to end the programme early without switching to Vienna at all.

We had an open control line to the Austrian Outside Broadcast Unit. Richard came on the line. 'Mike,' he said, 'don't give up. The pictures must come through soon. We *must* do this Outside Broadcast. It means so much to these people. For them to lose this chance to tell their story to the world would be a tragedy. Their story is all they have left.'

Two minutes later the Eurovision picture we had been waiting for flickered on to our monitors in the Lime Grove Studio. Within thirty seconds we had switched to Vienna and heard his familiar voice: 'This is Richard Dimbleby reporting for *Panorama* from Vienna, where to-night. . . .' We'd made it, and for the next twenty minutes he helped those Hungarian refugees tell their story to the world.

That is how I shall always remember Richard. A born reporter: full of heart and compassion; moved to action by the plight of the refugees, the homeless, the hungry; determined that their story should be told.

Respect for Facts

Many of the memorable Dimbleby broadcasts depended for their raw material on a flow of news – events such as Budget Days, major Parliamentary debates and above all, of course, the Elections from 1955 onwards. When I was in charge of the intake and channelling of news on such occasions I had my own special reasons for admiring and being grateful to Richard – as well as feeling deeply impressed, like everyone else, by all his other outstanding qualities on the job.

He had a thorough respect for the news facts of whatever he was presenting, and he was always prepared to take any amount of trouble in this cause. Often I've handed him a 'flash' reporting, say, the latest point in the Budget – on a strip of tape from the news agency teleprinter, with its own specialised abbreviations and with some annotations in hasty handwriting. Never any cause for anxiety: everyone could be absolutely confident that Richard would find his way through it all – and link it into its right context. The same, only more so, with Election news. Once, during a morning lull before the next spate of results, we were giving some news agency corrections to their original voting figures: nothing affecting the results – just a few emendations for the record. In one seat with a large majority there was a correction giving a losing candidate one more vote. I put this correction at the bottom of the others with a note on it: 'This might amuse you – no need to bother with it though!' Not at all: when Richard came to it, he gave the revised figures and added: 'Our apologies to the voter in this constituency whose vote I'm afraid we overlooked.'

One reason for this scrupulous regard for facts and news – however tense and exacting their presentation – was, I always felt, that Richard never forgot the beginning of his career as a news man.

General Election 1964 with David Butler (on his right), Ian Trethowan and Miren Cork

Ian Trethowan described Dimbleby's astonishing displays of mental and physical stamina on General Election nights in a tribute published in the 'Sunday Times':

Others might wilt, Richard kept indefatigably brisk. He had his own political views, but he made no claims to being a political animal. This was not necessarily a liability: at times he could cut through the maze of psephology with some devastatingly simple but appropriate plain man's question.

To those who worked with him, on those and other nights, any picture of him as humourless was ludicrous. Of course, he relished the pageantry and the aura of the State occasions. But at work, out of the camera's eye, he could be boisterously funny. In technical rehearsals, he would ease the tension by ambling cheerfully round the studio, joking with the studio crews, clutching a sheaf of indecipherable notes, getting himself caught up in microphone cables, until one wondered what on earth would happen 'on the night'.

Of course, 'on the night' one saw that every move had been carefully docketed away in his mind – and whenever anything went wrong, he was reassuringly certain how to put it right.

SIR GEOFFREY COX

A Reassuring Presence

One of Richard Dimbleby's remarkable qualities was his capacity not only of sustaining a high level of performance himself, but the rare one of being able to bring out the best in other people who appeared in programmes with him. I felt this strongly during the newspaper strike in April 1955. The BBC organised a panel of journalists who appeared during the evening to report on and discuss the news they would have written for their papers. At that time I was Assistant Editor of the *News Chronicle*, and was a member of this panel.

The first show was a mess. We had as chairman a man who was an excellent broadcaster himself, but who got the rest of us into a tangle again and again, cutting off nervous newcomers to the screen before they had made their points, switching the discussion along different lines to those previously agreed, and – the sin of sin – even taking over and using himself ideas which, at rehearsal, others said they would propound. But the next night Richard Dimbleby was in the chair, and the whole atmosphere – and with it the effectiveness of the broadcast – improved instantly.

He guided each speaker skilfully and sympathetically, drawing out clarification where someone had been a bit obscure, intervening to help those who were hesitant, carefully heading off those who tried to grab all the time. He did this partly by the reassurance of his presence and voice, but even more because he listened to what we had to say, and steered the contributions of each of us towards a unified and rounded programme. He appeared throughout genuinely interested in our facts and ideas, and this interest conveyed itself to the panel and the audience.

RICHARD DIMBLEBY

Listening in the Dark

They had the Garde Republicaine with all their lovely uniforms on the stairs and searchlights outside, something like a hundred and fifty thousand people outside the Opera House. I was in a box inside where I'd been for the performance, and had to commentate on her departure from the front of the Opera without seeing myself what was going on. I could see, of course, what the television cameras outside were showing me on a television set inside this box, so watching that I was able to describe the thing – that was the idea. Just before we went on – in fact, ten seconds before we went on the air – the lights failed in the Opera House, and not only was I plunged into pitch darkness but the monitor was switched off automatically and the picture went dead. The lights all went out and I was in this little box, with curtains across the front so dark that I literally couldn't see my hand if I held it up like this. Unable to see anything that was happening outside, but on the air – and since my telephone had broken down no means of telling the producer that I couldn't see, so I had to listen to the cheers outside and guess what was going on and say – 'Well now, here goes the procession', and with the sweat pouring down my face, and after about – after about ten minutes of this the producer realised that I couldn't see, and began telling me on my headphones what he could see through his cameras, and we managed to get it right. And I think people never really listen to television because nobody wrote in to say: 'Now what happened? What went wrong?' It was very disappointing. I wish somebody had noticed that we made a mess of it.

The Queen and Duke of Edinburgh with President René Coty at Paris Opera House, 8 April 1957

LEONARD MIALL

Monday Nights at Lime Grove

Through the eight years I was in charge of current affairs and talks pro-
grammes on BBC Television I spent most Monday evenings at Lime Grove.
That reconstructed old film studio seemed to acquire a special air of magical
excitement on Panorama nights. There was always a knot of schoolboys
with autograph books in the darkness outside the main door on the look-
out for visitors whose names were in that day's headlines, or would be in the
morrow's. Sometimes a senior Minister, sometimes an anonymous group
would come – for instance, women who were seen knitting throughout one
Panorama and then questioned on how much of the programme content they
had absorbed. One day in came a box filled with ice, into which a man was
locked, and he freed himself during transmission. Mrs Barbara Woodhouse
offered to give away to a good home a calf named Conquest, which we
watched snuggling down in a pen in the studio with her enormous and
beautifully trained Great Dane Juno. The Watford telephone exchange
was swamped with eager calls at the rate of 6,000 an hour.

You never knew what to expect. One day it was a French girl of nine
who was set the task of writing a poem on London at the beginning of the
programme. She was seen writing hard for a while, got up and bounced a
ball once or twice, went on writing, and Dimbleby finally put his excellent
French to use by translating the charming verse Minou Drouet had com-
posed. Another day there was a full-grown elephant in the fourth-floor
studio, carrying a man gently across the floor with its trunk.

With Minou Drouet

When we decided to make *Panorama* a weekly programme in 1955 I asked my deputy, Grace Wyndham Goldie, to supervise its new look. She immediately set on it that stamp of quality which marked all her television enterprises. It was she who first demanded that Richard Dimbleby should be the new anchorman, and before soon moving off to energise in turn the start of *Tonight* and then of *Monitor* she had firmly settled the guiding lines for *Panorama*: integrity in its coverage of current affairs, showmanship in its intelligent exploitation of the television medium.

The changing team of *Panorama* reporters have contributed a wide selection of talents. Most have had to be ready (as Dimbleby forecast even during the war for his two roving European reporters) to fly off at a moment's notice to where news was about to break. All have been interested in politics, some with one foot in it. Some left *Panorama* for the House of Commons, like Christopher Chataway and Woodrow Wyatt. Some came to *Panorama* after failing to be elected, like Robin Day and Ludovic Kennedy. Some combined journalism with a political past, like John Freeman and Angus Maude. There were ex-editors from Fleet Street, Malcolm Muggeridge and Francis Williams, and others whose background was essentially in broadcast journalism, Max Robertson, James Mossman, Michael Charlton, John Morgan, Michael Barratt, Ian Trethowan and Leonard Parkin. Others came and went. They were a talented and restless group, with a tendency to wish to leave after a few years, perhaps later to return again. *Panorama* reporters were welcomed by such world figures as President Kennedy, Pandit Nehru and the Shah of Persia. They were frequently involved themselves in controversy, for *Panorama* had to be involved in controversy, and they had to prise out cats which various vested interests preferred to keep in the bag.

In *Panorama*'s whirlpool, as Grace Wyndham Goldie has pointed out, Richard Dimbleby himself always managed to remain at the serene centre, not at the tumultuous edge. He did not want the reputation of a Robin Day or a Malcolm Muggeridge, and so, as she put it, 'he became on television a kind of living embodiment of stability, a reassuring symbol that somewhere at the heart of disturbance lies a basic kindliness and an enduring common sense'.

Panorama: clockwise, Rex Moorfoot (Editor), Dimbleby, Christopher Chataway, John Freeman, David Wheeler (Assistant Editor), Woodrow Wyatt, Christopher Burstall (Production Assistant), Margaret Douglas (Production Secretary)

With King Hussein of Jordan

The production teams were constantly turning over, as inventive production assistants and producers, trained in the hard school of Panorama, went off to produce new programmes of their own.

Michael Peacock was the first of several editors, each of whom brought some special attribute to Panorama: Rex Moorfoot, Michael Peacock again, after a spell with Outside Broadcasts, Paul Fox, David Wheeler and now Jeremy Isaacs.

Richard Dimbleby remained the one constant factor. He would arrive on Monday mornings and go very carefully through the elaborate studio moves, which were never the same from one programme to the next. A length of film needs to run for eight seconds on a television projector (telecine) before it reaches full speed. An anchorman has to be able to cue the start of the telecine machine and then speak for exactly eight seconds. Dimbleby was impeccable. He would finger his spectacles, indicating the start of the eight seconds, and finish his sentence invariably just as the first frame came up – or if it was late in coming he would spin out his words until out of the corner of his eye he saw the picture arrive on his monitor. He enjoyed demonstrating maps and summarising complicated situations. 'Let me see if I can simplify it' he would say, and one felt he was a teacher manqué as well as a surgeon manqué.

His long apprenticeship in radio had made him a master at reading a prepared commentary to a film sequence, and he could get through a last-minute session in the Lime Grove dubbing theatre much faster than most, for his readings were always right first time.

After a day of very careful preparation he changed his clothes and ate a light supper. He would then greet, and set at ease, the important, and the unimportant, and the often temperamental protagonists we had invited to the studio. Dimbleby was invariably an excellent host, and Panorama's guests were always anxious to meet him. So too were many distinguished visitors to London such as King Hussein of Jordan, who dined with us one night because he wished to see television in action. We took him on a tour of the studios, and finally ended up in Panorama, where a memorable interview took place with the King and Dimbleby, like Johnson and Boswell, each calling the other 'Sir' in every sentence.

H.R.H. the Duke of Edinburgh had introduced the International Geo-physical Year on television, and reported on his travels in a children's pro-gramme. The first time that he, or any other of the Queen's immediate family, decided to allow himself to be questioned on a regular current affairs programme was at the hands of Richard Dimbleby.

There were occasions when Dimbleby almost acted as a national Ombuds-man, or a restorer of national confidence. When the world was on the brink of nuclear war over Cuba, and Panorama was mounting a special pro-gramme, a woman telephoned to say she would send her children to school only if Richard Dimbleby said it was safe. He made a point of saying to an authority in the studio, 'I am aware that a great many people today are extremely worried and frightened by what has happened, and have some awful feeling that something dreadful may happen quite quickly, suddenly. Do you think there is reason at all for short-term immediate nerves on this?'

There were several occasions when he was game to subject himself to any kind of treatment in the studio, be it an ice-cream tasting contest with Francis Williams to guess which was made with real cream, or being flung around the studio in an aircraft seat on wheels to test the shock of sudden braking, or swallowing a tiny transmitter and picking up the signals from inside his massive frame, or being spun round in a space simulator at the RAF Medical Centre. For the last programme before Panorama's much needed annual summer break in 1959, he demonstrated the new American craze for balloon jumping from an airfield at Weston-on-the-Green. It was fascinating to watch his considerable mass reduced to nothing as his weight was counterbalanced by a balloon on his shoulders, and Dimbleby leapt ten to fifteen feet in the air and covered the same distance between strides along the ground.

He had his little vanities. One was getting the make-up assistant to black the balding patch on the back of his head, until it could no longer be disguised. In the studio there was always fun with the technical crew. Dur-ing a programme which demonstrated the gimmicks of the 1964 American Election campaign, Dimbleby opened a bottle of Barry Goldwater Cologne for Men. An electrician chargehand next to him commented on the pungent

aroma, and asked if it was coming from him. Dimbleby put the neck of the bottle against the chargehand's arm meaning to 'spot' him, but accidentally poured a large quantity on to him. The electrician washed it off but the smell remained strong. After the programme he declared that when he got home his wife would ask searching questions as to the origin of the perfume. Dimbleby immediately wrote a note on a page of his script:

'Dear Jackie,

This is to certify that I, Richard Dimbleby, have soaked your husband in Barry Goldwater Cologne. He is concerned in case you suspect him of wrong doings.

Personally I think it improves the brute.

Regards,
RICHARD.'

Dimbleby used to keep the studio crews in fits of laughter with earthy stories, mostly unprintable. There was wonderful teamwork, and constant banter, between him and Joan Marsden, Panorama's regular floor manager. The floor manager wears a receiver on the belt with headphones to pick up the director's instructions and pass them on to the studio performers. During an edition of Panorama from Sotheby's sale room which was beamed to America by Early Bird, Joan raised her finger to give Richard the customary 'one minute' cue. As soon as he had finished that particular link and a piece of film was running he beckoned her over and said, 'For Heaven's sake don't do that or you will find yourself having bought a picture for £10,000 – "Sold to the lady with the double deaf aid!".'

She is one of many people for whom Monday nights at Lime Grove have lost something of their magic.

Inaugural programme, Early Bird, with Joan Marsden

When Richard Cawston came to join the production team of Panorama from Film Department he brought with him a scheme which had long been cherished by Charles de Jaeger, a cameraman with a Viennese background. De Jaeger, who seemed to have relations in every capital of Europe, as well as an outsize sense of humour, wanted to make a visual April Fool's joke about a spaghetti harvest. The proposal never got anywhere until Cawston arrived at Panorama and then it had to wait until 1 April came on a Monday. In 1957 it did. Charles de Jaeger was on another assignment in Switzerland near Lugano. He stuck twenty pounds of spaghetti on to laurel bushes with sellotape and photographed it from every angle. All of us involved with Panorama, and Richard himself, felt it was high time that television was taken with some critical scepticism. David Wheeler wrote a script and Richard put it over dead pan. As the film opened with shots of burgeoning buds, Richard said:

RICHARD DIMBLEBY

Spaghetti Harvest

Monday

1

April

1957

It isn't only in Britain that spring this year has taken everyone by surprise. Here, in the Ticino, on the borders of Switzerland and Italy, the slopes overlooking Lake Lugano have already burst into flower, at least a fortnight earlier than usual. But what – you may ask – has the early and welcome arrival of bees and blossoms to do with food? Well, it's simply that the past winter, one of the mildest in living memory, has had its effect in other ways as well. Most important of all, it's resulted in an exceptionally heavy spaghetti crop. The last two weeks of March are an anxious time for the spaghetti farmer. There's always the chance of a late frost which – while not entirely ruining the crop, generally impairs the flavour, and makes it difficult for him to obtain top prices in world markets. But now these dangers are over, and the spaghetti harvest goes forward.

Spaghetti cultivation here in Switzerland is not, of course, carried out on anything like the tremendous scale of the Italian industry. Many of you, I'm sure, will have seen pictures of the vast spaghetti plantations in the Po Valley. For the Swiss, however, it tends to be more of a family affair. Another reason why this may be a bumper year lies in the virtual disappearance of the spaghetti weevil, the tiny creature whose depredations have caused much concern in the past.

After picking, the spaghetti is laid out to dry in the warm Alpine sun. Many people are often puzzled by the fact that spaghetti is produced at such uniform lengths, but this is the result of many years of patient endeavour by plant breeders who have succeeded in producing the perfect spaghetti. And now the harvest is marked by a traditional meal. Toasts to the new crop are drunk in these poccalinos, and then the waiters enter bearing the ceremonial dish, and it is, of course, spaghetti, picked earlier in the day, dried in the sun and so brought fresh from garden to table at the very peak of condition. For those who love this dish there's nothing like real home-grown spaghetti.

The film ended with Swiss in national costume tucking into the meal and

we came back to a shot of Richard at his Panorama desk closing the programme.

We had arranged for an outsize calendar to be on his desk proclaiming I April and Richard said: 'and that is all from Panorama on this first day of April'. Nevertheless, a very large number of people were hoaxed. I went to the BBC's telephone exchange in Lime Grove where for the next two hours calls came in incessantly. Some were from viewers who had enjoyed the joke, including one from Bristol who complained 'spaghetti doesn't grow vertically, it grows horizontally'. But mainly they came with the request that the BBC should settle a family argument. The husband knew it must be true that spaghetti grew on a bush because Dimbleby had said it. The wife knew that spaghetti was made with flour and water. Neither could convince the other.

I had thought it wise to inform the Director-General of the BBC, Sir Ian Jacob, beforehand that this hoax was due to be perpetrated in a current affairs programme. Unfortunately, someone forgot to pass my message on. I ran into Sir Ian two days later at Broadcasting House. He said: 'I always used to think that monkey nuts grew on bushes until I went to serve in the Canal Zone and saw them growing on the ground. The moment I saw the spaghetti item on Panorama, I said to my wife, "I'm sure spaghetti doesn't grow on a bush." We had to look up three books before we confirmed it.'

By 30 September 1957 Richard Dimbleby had completed twenty-one years of broadcasting. In Panorama that evening he took stock of his career in a self-interview by asking questions of his image fed from another camera on to a television screen:

RICHARD DIMBLEBY

Twenty-one Years of Broadcasting

Question: Mr Dimbleby, you began broadcasting twenty-one years ago. How many broadcasts – radio or television, all put together – do you think you've done in that time?

Answer: Well, I've tried to add it up – I think it must be in the region of – it's approaching three thousand.

Question: Well, out of those three thousand are there any particular ones that you remember more than any other?

Answer: Yes, I think there are – I think there are five. The first one was 1938 – these are all occasions on which I was commentator or present – 1938 when Chamberlain came back to Heston Airport, the height of the Munich crisis, waving in his hand a little bit of paper and saying 'This means peace in our time', if you remember; and then the first

report from the Western Front in the Second World War, that the BEF had gone into action against the German Army, I happened to give that one myself. And later on in the war the discovery of the Belsen concentration camp, I was among the first three people who went in through the gates of that camp, something so horrible I'll never forget it. Much later on the Coronation of our Queen, because I think that was a great occasion, for television, apart from all its other implications. And more recently, a couple of years ago, the marathon general election television broadcast when we seemed to go on for about twenty-one hours on end without stopping.

Question: Now if I may ask you just one or two pointed questions about yourself and hope for a frank answer. It has been said by people that you're only really happy in what you're doing and only really successful in what you're doing when you're mixing with dukes and you're messing about in stately homes. What have you got to say to that?

Answer: Well, it's absolute nonsense to start with. I have had to do quite a lot of these 'At Home' programmes for the BBC, which does involve going into stately homes, and in stately homes you are apt to find dukes, you can't help that. You find lots of other people too, commoners as well. If the Duke is lively and the stately home's a beautiful one, I'm perfectly happy, but I'm no more at home there than I am anywhere else. In the course of my twenty-one years I've been all over the country, I've interviewed everybody under the sun, I've always felt welcome and I've always felt perfectly at home. Duke or dustman or anyone else, I don't mind who it is.

Question: Well, would you answer this – the critics frequently say that you are pompous. What about that?

Answer: Now that's something that makes me livid. Look, I don't think that they know, half of 'em, the difference between pomp and weight. In all the years that I worked in radio and wasn't seen, nobody ever said I was pompous. The moment I appear on a television screen, they say – He's pompous. I know what it is, they see I'm enormous – I can't help that, I am – and because I'm heavy and large they think that heavy and large people are pompous. If I may say so, it's exactly the same thing as when they say that I'm talking in reverential hushed whispers – I daresay you've read that quite often. The reason very often being that on a State occasion or a big occasion, a lot of which I've had the good fortune to do for the BBC as a commentator, on those occasions if you're in a large hushed hall during a solemn ceremony you can't exactly shout in a Light Programme type of voice, or you'd drown the ceremony and bring it to a standstill. That's the only reason why I ever whisper anywhere – it's not reverence, it's pure necessity.

Question: Well, what about the critics – have you any views on them?

Answer: That's a temptation. Critics – in my opinion there are only four real television critics in Great Britain. The rest are newspaper reporters who've turned to television as a change from crime.

Question: Well, now I'll ask you, if I may, the sixty-four thousand dollar question – the last one – and it's this – I'm sorry, you can't do that, time's up.

Answer: Yes, well, you're quite right, so it is.

At Woburn Abbey with the Duke of Bedford

F

The State Opening of Parliament

When Richard died, I had worked with him for over six years as a *Panorama* colleague, and had got to know him very well through innumerable Monday conversations enlivened by his earthy humour, his caustic comments on *Panorama* items he disliked, and his endearing love of uninhibited gossip. But I first met Richard not as a colleague but as a rival – this was in 1958 – when I was working for ITV. This gave me my first inside knowledge of his professional skill and his friendly courtesy.

The occasion was a historic one for both television and Parliament. The State Opening of Parliament by Her Majesty the Queen, a ceremony second only in splendour and solemnity to the Coronation, was to be televised for the first time. At half-past nine in the morning I climbed up through a trap-door into a wooden cubicle smaller than a telephone kiosk. It had been installed high up between the Victorian Gothic arches of the House of Lords chamber. The small glass window looked across the golden Throne at the other end. A few feet away from me, in a companion cubicle, Richard Dimbleby had squeezed into his position. He was to provide the commentary for BBC viewers; I was the ITV commentator. 'Dimbleby *v.* Day' was the theme of Press comments, or, as the *Daily Express* put it, 'The Gentleman versus the Chap'.

This was an assignment in which practically everything was against me. I was a novice competing with the master craftsman, a man who knew from countless royal occasions every jewel in the Imperial Crown and every stitch on a herald's tabard. The TV pictures were being provided by the BBC and 'fed' to ITV. This put me in the awkward position of having to comment on a sequence of pictures selected by a producer who was following Richard's words. Supposing, for instance, that Peter Dimmock, the BBC producer, had shown a shot of King George V's statue and was about to go to a shot of the Victoria Tower. Richard would be saying 'and there is the memorial to the Queen's grandfather, the beloved Sailor King'. Dimmock, whose camera instructions were heard on headphones by Richard and myself, would shout 'coming to Victoria Tower'. At this, Richard would skilfully wind up his remarks about King George V and lead into a shot of the Victoria Tower, like this: 'the beloved Sailor King, George V, whose statue stands across the road opposite the great Victoria Tower'. Meanwhile I would be trying to do the same thing. The difficulty was that though Richard Dimbleby was, like myself, following Peter Dimmock's cues, the exact moment at which Dimmock put a given picture on the screen would be timed to fit Richard's words. As soon as Richard got to the word 'Victoria', up would come the tower on the screen. The BBC provided me with details of the order and timing of the shots to be taken by their cameras. Even so, it was pure luck whether my words fitted the pictures as closely as Richard's. It was an exceedingly tricky business to

form appropriate phrases with the roar of the crowds and bands in one ear, and Dimmock shouting his control-room instructions in the other: 'Coming to Horse Guards Arch – where are you, Camera Seven? . . . Coming to Horse Guards Arch now . . . Hurry up, Richard . . .', with Richard's commentary somewhere in the background.

Another problem facing me was that of style. Only the BBC had been allowed to install cameras, but the ITV network had been given the right to have their own commentator. It was made clear to me that something different from the Dimbleby style was required. It was not made clear how this difference was to be achieved. How *could* one be very different in tone from Richard when describing a solemn royal occasion? Yet any attempt to imitate or outdo the master with majestic, flowing descriptions was doomed to failure.

During the preparations and rehearsals I met him several times, and if he regarded me as a somewhat brash and bumptious rival, he did not show it. He could not have been more helpful to me, though the occasion was one of the first big state occasions in which ITV had shared and Richard was naturally determined that the BBC would score a triumph. He never failed to pass on to me any point I would need to know. During my researches I was trying to locate an expert description of the elaborately ornamented throne – on which the camera was to dwell frequently. Eventually it appeared that the most authoritative and detailed description was in Richard's hands. He readily sent me a copy, with his good wishes.

One tiny incident demonstrated to me his professional skill and experience. It had been arranged during rehearsals that at a certain point in the ceremony the cameras would dwell for a few moments on the pictures along one wall of the Royal Gallery, and I had duly memorised all necessary details of the monarchs or consorts whose portraits might be seen. Alas, when the time came the cameras had, for some unexpected reason, to focus on a completely different set of pictures hanging on the opposite wall. This did not throw Richard in the slightest. Though he did not go into names or details, his commentary flowed calmly on with appropriate references of a general kind. But I was so irritated at the unexpected change of plan that instead of continuing as best I could, I banged down the commentator's 'cut-off' switch and cursed. My 'covering' reference came to mind too late and I regret to say that for several silent and embarrassing seconds a portrait of one of Her Majesty's ancestors, whom I did not recognise, filled the screen undescribed and unidentified. A trivial incident – and one which few people noticed – but it made me very angry with myself at the time, and humbly envious of the veteran's skill.

Some years later I happened to be doing the BBC commentary on President Kennedy's inauguration. This was a ceremony which Richard would normally have covered, but for some accidental reason which I cannot recall, the assignment fell to me. He watched the broadcast with a keen professional eye, and the following Monday we discussed it in detail. From the TV commentator's standpoint the Inaugural had been a chaotic business and my commentary must have revealed this. Richard, however, was full of a fellow professional's

understanding: 'I could see what your problem was at that point' or
'I know exactly what you were up against when so-and-so happened'.
And his verdict was very generous, which was typical.

*In October 1959 the Dimblebys went to Buckingham Palace for Richard
to receive from the hands of the Duke of Edinburgh the CBE which he
had been awarded in the Birthday Honours List. He had already been the
winner of many national radio and television awards.*

*Not everyone took to Dimbleby's prose style, which John Crosby, the
London-based columnist of the 'New York Herald Tribune', once attempted
to convey to his American readers thus:*

And now, as the leaves are turning to gold and the glittering draughts
of campaign oratory turn sere and yellow in the newspaper files, let us
turn our attention to the majestic cadences of Richard Dimbleby's prose,
which may have permanently affected my own and gives even this opening sentence, if I make so bold, a resplendent thunder, a faint but distant
echo of Mr Dimbleby's own glorious, and if I may, and on the whole I
don't know why I shouldn't say, gleaming utterances. But, my God,
Dimbleby, how in hell do you ever get the damned sentences to stop
once you get them rolling along like this?

From Russia with Dimbleby

Until the death of Stalin in 1953 the cold war numbed broadcasting relations between the Soviet Union and Great Britain. British camera teams were not allowed to enter Russia. Correspondents were denied visas. Broadcasts in the BBC's European Service were systematically jammed. There were none of the normal interchanges of musical programmes or sporting events between broadcasting organisations.

In 1956 a slight thaw began. The Russians sent an engineer to observe the BBC's experimental colour television demonstrations at Alexandra Palace. When Khrushchev and Bulganin came to visit Sir Anthony Eden in April of that year the idea of cultural exchanges was mooted. As a first step they invited an official delegation from the BBC to come and inspect radio and television in Moscow, Leningrad and Kiev.

By the end of April, even before Bulganin and Khrushchev had sailed back to Russia, seven of us representing BBC Sound and Television, Engineering and Programmes, External Services and News, had flown to Moscow, just in time to see the famous May Day parade through Red Square. Anatol Goldberg, the Programme Organiser of the BBC's Russian section, was able to interpret for us. The Russians also provided as a guide and interpreter Boris Belitzky, who was one of the regular broadcasters in Moscow Radio's English service. Belitzky had lived in New York as a boy and spoke excellent English. He left us on May Day to give the English language radio commentary on the parade. The Russian television service was also developing, and the parade was televised for the first time that year, with two outside broadcast units on opposite sides of Red Square. The broadcast was technically impressive, though the cameras were badly placed.

We had many discussions with the Russians, seeking ways of opening up broadcasting relationships without the sacrifice of principle on matters such as censorship, and without involving either of us in carrying the other's propaganda. The discussions tended to founder when we brought up the question of jamming. Russians love metaphors and elaborate figures of speech, and so at one of their many hospitable occasions the Director of External Services, J. B. Clark, made a glowing speech about the beautiful garden which lay ahead, 'but the gates of the garden have their hinges and locks corroded by jamming'. The Soviet Deputy Minister of Communications quickly replied, 'The gates must be open, but the key to the gates must be in the pocket of the master of the garden'.

Nevertheless Frank Gillard, who was representing Sound Programmes, and I, representing Television, did return with one positive achievement. We had got the names of two broadcasters speaking excellent English who would be prepared to take part (in sound only) in hook-up discussions of current affairs, subject to official permission. One was Yuri Fokin, soon to become Head of News of Moscow Radio. The other was Boris Belitzky. This represented substantial progress, for the Russians at that time had no tradition of unscripted discussion at all. Moreover we returned with their

Brussels International Exhibition, 1958, with Boris Belitzky, Sir John Balfour, U.K. Commissioner-General, Model Sputnik III

Soviet cameras, a Flemish outside broadcast, the Eurovision link, standards conversion and photographed off the television screen

telephone numbers, and had learned that the telephone appeared to pierce the Iron Curtain fairly easily. We also broached the question of a possible television hook-up as soon as the links across Europe could be established. At that time the Russians had not yet even linked Moscow with Leningrad.

Belitzky had welcomed the idea of contributing in sound only to Panorama. He knew Dimbleby well by voice and reputation. As soon as the Russians launched their first Sputnik I telephoned Moscow and in the next Panorama Belitzky's voice took part in the studio discussion of the possibility of the space age.

In 1958 the television hook-up with Moscow moved one stage closer. At the International Exhibition at Brussels the Soviet Pavilion was equipped with closed circuit television. With the aid of a Flemish outside broadcast unit and the Eurovision link Dimbleby was able to introduce a BBC programme with the words 'I am speaking to you direct from a studio of Radio Moscow'. He liked dramatic openings and this was literally true, for Radio Moscow had provided the television studio and cameras in the Soviet Pavilion.

Richard Dimbleby and Boris Belitzky, meeting face to face for the first time, then toured the Soviet Pavilion and talked to an attractive interpreter, Maya Malisheva, who displayed fur coats and Russian food delicacies, including one item that intrigued Dimbleby – porridge for dessert. It was a highly complicated programme for the BBC producer, Derek Burrell-Davis, for he was dealing with a Russian outside broadcast unit, a Flemish outside broadcast unit, and a Russian telecine machine, and the technical crews had no common language.

British viewers and television critics were fascinated by their first live view of Soviet activity. The 'Guardian' television critic commented: 'A complicated broadcast which was well handled by Derek Burrell-Davis, the British producer, and by Richard Dimbleby, who had abandoned his baronial manner very successfully under the shadow of Lenin, and who did not forget to remind us, as the camera passed finally from sucking pig, salmon, chickens, sturgeons, mutton chops and porridge-for-dessert to a last glimpse of Sputnik III, that "there is always something like that looking down on you".'

I was interested to note the next evening in Brussels that Flemish television repeated exactly the same programme for Belgian viewers, with one of their own commentators taking Dimbleby's place, and a Flemish-speaking Russian instead of Belitzky. But they stuck entirely to the shape of the programme carefully prepared by Dimbleby and Burrell-Davis and did not even bother to issue another camera script to the technical crew. The Dimbleby moves and the Dimbleby questions could not be improved upon.

Peter Dimmock wrote to the Russian authorities warmly thanking them for their co-operation and hoping for further opportunities for the outside broadcast units of the two countries to work together in the future.

Other BBC visitors travelled to Moscow. Aubrey Singer went in search of scientific programme material, Peter Dimmock to arrange film of the USA/USSR athletics match. Dimmock reported that the Russians were hoping to create a television link with Prague via Warsaw in order to be able to receive the 1960 Olympic Games live from Rome. We continued to work for a live hook-up from Moscow. At the same time discussions went on from *time to time to try to abolish jamming. Dimmock reported that the Russians were beginning to favour ITV on the film coverage of sport, because, as ITV did not broadcast to Russia, there were no complications over jamming.*

In February 1960 the Soviet Union ceased its jamming of the BBC's European programmes, and this obstacle seemed out of the way. Early the next year ATV proudly announced that they were going to achieve the first television link-up from Moscow to Britain, by live coverage of the British Trade Exhibition, due to open in Moscow on 17 May 1961, and even took advertising space in British newspapers and periodicals to publish the announcement in Russian.

After all the BBC's pioneering work on Eurovision, and its long negotiations with the Russians, this was too clear a challenge to be ignored. The BBC countered with an offer to relay the morning May Day parade from Moscow that year and, because 1 May fell on a Monday, to broadcast that evening a special edition of Panorama from Moscow. Richard Dimbleby would do both programmes. The Russian authorities agreed. Peter Dimmock and Tony Bridgewater, then the senior engineer on the outside broadcasting side, went to Moscow, and with generous help from the Russians and the Finns worked out a method of getting the Moscow pictures across the Baltic from Tallin to Helsinki, and so down the Eurovision link through Scandinavia to Britain. Paul Fox flew to Moscow to prepare the Panorama programme, Noble Wilson to arrange the relay of the May Day Parade. Paul Fox recalls:

Filled with doubts, I arrived in Moscow to arrange the *Panorama* side of things. Already installed in the National Hotel was Noble Wilson. And as we looked at our plans for this first-timer from Russia, something far bigger overtook us. A friend – an American correspondent – phoned us with the news that something was on: he couldn't tell what. And even as we puzzled it out, the loudspeakers blared into action: 'The Soviet Union has today launched the first man into space'.

Major Yuri Gagarin was circling the globe. And soon afterwards came the news that he was safely back – with Moscow getting ready for the hero's welcome of all time.

Here we were, two television producers, sitting in on the most spectacular story for many a year, with not a hope of televising a second of it to the rest of Europe. What an anticlimax the May Day parade would be – we thought – when the Gagarin home-coming and parade was what everyone wanted to see. But was it really hopeless? Could not the much planned television link-up for May Day be brought forward by seventeen days? It might be and it was.

I was in my Lime Grove office on the evening of 13 April when Paul Fox came through on the telephone from Moscow to say he thought he had managed to get the programme through to Helsinki in time for the broadcast of Gagarin's return to Moscow Airport the very next morning. I immediately announced to the press, and we began trailing heavily on both sound and television the news that we hoped to cover the Gagarin reception – the first man to travel in space, and the first live television pictures from Moscow. It could only be a hope, for official Soviet approval had not yet been given, and we had had no chance to test reception conditions.

I quickly telephoned Dimbleby, who dropped his other commitments to

come in the next morning. I also corralled Anatol Goldberg from the BBC's Russian Service, and at 10.30 a.m. on Friday 14 April we opened transmission.

Dimbleby explained, as he enjoyed explaining technicalities in layman's language, the complications of getting pictures along the route from Moscow to London. We showed what little news film had come in from Russia, and Dimbleby and Goldberg talked in the studio for a quarter of an hour as we anxiously waited for pictures on the studio monitor. At 10.46 a.m. they miraculously came through, and television was now stretching from Moscow to Londonderry.

The pictures were remarkably good, but the sound was confused. Sometimes we heard a man in Helsinki, sometimes Boris Belitzky. Dimbleby thrived on confusions of that kind, and Gagarin's walk across the apron of Moscow Airport to receive the bearhug embrace of Khrushchev needed no words of commentary.

Dimbleby had been there to open yet another chapter in television's unfolding story. A few days later he flew off to broadcast in quick succession the May Day parade, Panorama's special edition from Moscow, and the Queen's State visit to Italy.

NOBLE WILSON

Moscow — May 1961

It was 27 April 1961: four days before the first live television relay to Western Europe of the celebrated May Day Parade from Red Square, Moscow. Quite apart from the technical and political problems which had kept many of us active for months beforehand, this was as difficult and delicate a commentary as any that Richard had faced in his broadcasting career. It became all the more of a challenge when we learned that as a result of meetings in London it had been agreed that his commentary on the parade was to be shared with Boris Belitzky of Moscow Radio.

Richard was not pleased with the decision, but his irritation only showed itself in the extra colourful and pithy comments on life in general and Soviet waiters in particular during the two and a half hours that it took them to serve us dinner. He understood full well the pressures at work, and as on so many occasions, quietly stifled thoughts of self. He also knew and liked Belitzky. However, although it had been decided in principle that he and Boris should share the commentary, there was no ruling on how this was to be done. We had our views; the Soviet Television authorities were bound to have theirs; just twenty-four hours before transmission we met to talk about it in an office on the first floor of the barrack-like Television Centre.

The Chairman of the meeting was Konstantin Kuzakov, the Director of Television. With him was Yuri Fokin, the Head of News and principal commentator, and a number of others. But the focus was on just two men: Dimbleby and Belitzky. The latter, feeling slightly uncomfortable, a radio man directed to work in the relatively unfamiliar medium of television on a programme of considerable political importance; the former, shadow-boxing gently as the pleasantries were exchanged, sniffing the political air, sizing up the problem. And the rest of us sat around them like so many seconds out of the ring.

The meeting ground on in the way that meetings do in Moscow, until Kuzakov said that he was sure the best thing would be if the two commentators went to another office and settled the matter by themselves. Richard, with a quick 'Don't worry' look at me, got up and said, 'Splendid idea – come on, Boris, or we won't get any lunch'.

Somewhere in the Soviet archives there may be a recording of what Richard said to Boris and what Boris said to Richard, both surely conscious that they were not alone. Richard told me later that it was all very polite but formal. After about an hour, they came back to Kuzakov's office and told us how they intended to 'divide' the parade between them. There were some parts which still worried me, but on the whole it seemed that honour on both sides had been satisfied.

Boris and Richard and I lunched together at the Praga restaurant, all of us, I think, relieved that official needs had been met. It was very much a working lunch, with Richard asking question after question. Boris was weak on some of the military details but knew the parade well and was able to provide a lot of information about the personalities taking part. He was altogether very helpful to Richard and told me privately that he had a great respect for him as a broadcaster.

Although Richard had managed to secure the commentary on most of the politically tricky parts of the parade, there was still one item which worried us. At a certain point, workers from a locomotive factory were due to march on with garlands and banners bearing such slogans as 'Hands Off Cuba' and 'Down with American Imperialism'. And this part was to be covered by Boris.

That evening we checked circuits and lines and microphones, while Richard settled down to his homework. At 2.30 a.m. he was still working on the names of the Soviet Praesidium, calling them out as John Drummond held up their photographs. It was like some weird Russian parlour game – goodness knows what a listening monitor may have made of *that* night's tape!

After a very few hours' sleep, we all gathered at the breakfast bar on our floor. Richard was cheerful, with an edge of determination glinting through the banter. As usual, we had an interminable wait for the lift – Richard said he was certain that waiting for lifts was the principal reason why Russians read Dostoyevsky novels. After a car ride down Gorki Street, and a brief argument with the police cordon, we reached our room on the top floor of GUM, which, as every tourist knows, is the biggest department store in Moscow, and which runs along one side of Red Square, opposite the Kremlin. It was not an ideal commentary position – the windows were narrow and restricted the view to left and right. But it was directly opposite the saluting base on Lenin's tomb, and there was plenty of room for notes and scripts. It was also warm, comfortable and well equipped.

Richard and Boris were in a sort of commentary booth near the window, screened by drapes and glass from the rest of the room. Each had a monitor in front of him and there was an on/off switch for the micro-

The Kremlin

and the Belfry of Ivan the Terrible

St Nicholas Church, Moscow

Opposite: The May Day parade from Moscow, with Dimbleby in front of St Basil's Cathedral in Red Square, and Marshal Malinovsky, Minister of Defence, taking the salute with Khrushchev and Gagarin

In Red Square

phones. From a control position I had talk-back to Richard and Boris as well as communication with London. But there was little I could do now – it was all up to Richard and the pictures from the Soviet cameras. I was still concerned about Boris and those slogans. Of course I needn't have worried. I should have remembered that in 1945 it was Richard who made a Russian patrol in Berlin release him by persuading them that he was a son of Winston Churchill. Instead of stopping his commentary, Richard 'missed the place' and went straight on, translating the slogans without emphasis and attracting attention to more interesting things. Then he switched off the mike, turned to Boris and said, 'Oh, I'm terribly sorry, Boris, you were supposed to do that bit.' Clearly, it wasn't Boris's fault.

Every instinct he had was at concert pitch that morning. Every word was carefully chosen and placed. I remember one particular moment when, at the end of the military parade, the 'spontaneous demonstration' of citizens of Moscow began. Across the square they came in their thousands, untidy and shuffling. It would have been all too easy to use the wrong verb: 'shambling' would have been too strong – 'walking' too weak. Richard used 'ambling' and somehow managed to make it sound as scruffy as it looked.

That evening we saw Richard off on the Comet back to London; but not to rest – by the very next morning he had to be in Naples to give a commentary on the arrival of Her Majesty the Queen and the Duke of Edinburgh at the start of their State Visit to Italy. There was not even time to go home, so a room in one of the airport hotels had been booked to allow him to relax for a few hours: and so that he could watch his own *Panorama* he'd arranged for a television set to be specially installed. With his mind still echoing with the events of a memorable May Day, Richard began to concentrate on the next task ahead. There were also letters to be signed and private business to be discussed during these hours between flights. Yet he found time to telephone each of our families and assure them that all was well with us – but then Richard, always and instinctively, found time for kindness.

LEONARD MIALL

Meet Major Gagarin

As a reciprocal gesture the Russians agreed to relay the Trooping the Colour, and Yuri Fokin came to London to speak the Russian commentary, following on headphones what Richard Dimbleby was saying. Dimbleby always briefed the European commentators carefully before any major event, and greatly eased their tasks for them. A month later Major Gagarin unexpectedly came to Britain to appear at the Soviet Exhibition at Earl's Court.

On Tuesday 11 July 1961, Dimbleby was at London Airport to describe his arrival. Gagarin was met by the Soviet Ambassador, the Deputy Chief of the Air Staff, and a civil servant, the secretary to the Minister of Science, Lord Hailsham. Dimbleby was also the commentator later that day at a televised press conference from the Earl's Court Exhibition, a curious affair at which much of the questioning was puerile, and some speakers from Eastern Europe insisted on reading out poems to the cosmonaut. Belitzky was again doing the translating, and Dimbleby complained on the air that he thought the arrangements at London Airport for greeting the first man to travel in space had been inadequate. A member of the Government and not a civil servant should have been there.

There was in fact a lively debate in Britain on the degree of welcome which should be extended to Gagarin, for this was a period of some political tension in Anglo-Soviet affairs. It was soon resolved by the Queen inviting Gagarin to one of her informal luncheon parties on the Friday of that week.

Meanwhile some newspapers charged that the BBC was departing from its charter by taking sides in a current controversy, and I told our press office to point out that Richard was expressing his own view, which he was perfectly entitled to do. The BBC as such was not, as alleged, taking an editorial line. The 'Daily Herald' and some others made out that the BBC was annoyed with Dimbleby and was publicly repudiating him. This in turn made the new Director-General, Hugh Carleton Greene, angry, and he took the trouble to telephone Dimbleby to assure him personally that the papers had got it all wrong. Dimbleby, who had at that time not met the new Director-General, much appreciated the telephone call.

Meanwhile we were trying to arrange a proper television interview at which Gagarin could be questioned. Paul Fox was handling the negotiations with Rogov of the Soviet Embassy. After several conversations on Thursday 13 July, the Russians agreed, provided that Yuri Fokin could be part of the panel, and that the general areas of questioning, though not specific questions, should be submitted in writing as soon as possible. This was accepted and we prepared announcements to say that a special programme 'Meet Major Gagarin' would be recorded at the Soviet Exhibition the next day and transmitted later that evening in place of a Burns and Allen programme. Richard Dimbleby would be the chairman, Tom Margerison, Science Editor of the 'Sunday Times', would be on the panel with Yuri Fokin, and Boris Belitzky would be the interpreter.

Meanwhile the British Government had changed its official attitude towards Gagarin. On that Thursday I went to a hastily arranged reception for him at the Hyde Park Hotel. The Prime Minister, Mr Macmillan, the Foreign Secretary, Lord Home, and the Minister of Science, Lord Hailsham, were all there.

Later that evening Lord Hailsham came to Lime Grove to appear on Gallery. While we were talking with him and Lady Hailsham after the programme Paul Fox phoned. He said that, despite the earlier agreement, Rogov had just been instructed to insist that unless every single question to be put to Gagarin was submitted in writing by 9.30 the next morning the programme was off. I told Fox that in that case the programme would have to be off. Distinguished broadcasters like Margerison and Dimbleby could never agree to submit all their questions in advance. Nor could the BBC. But I also told him to warn the Soviet Embassy that we would have to announce why the broadcast was cancelled. I also asked Fox to go round to the Soviet Embassy the next morning to try to get them to return to the earlier agreement.

Fox telephoned the next morning to say all was well. The Embassy had *withdrawn its demand for written questions in advance. Gagarin with Belitzky as interpreter went to lunch at Buckingham Palace, and came straight on to the room in the Earl's Court Exhibition where we had set up our cameras.*

Gagarin entered accompanied by the Soviet Ambassador, who was in a bad temper, and General Kaminin, the Russian in charge of space experiments. There was also a large collection of very tough-looking security men. Dimbleby greeted them all courteously.

The discussion went very well. Gagarin had great charm and answered easily. At the end, just as Dimbleby had been given a 'Three minutes more' sign by the floor manager, Fokin stepped in with a very long and heavily polemical statement only just in the form of a question. Gagarin gave an equally long political reply. Dimbleby wasn't going to end on that note, so he quickly asked Gagarin what presents he was proposing to take back to Moscow. There was a hurried consultation with Belitzky, who replied, 'Major Gagarin is going to take back toys for his children, souvenirs of London, and something for his wife which he will not disclose, in order that it may remain a secret.' It was in fact a fur coat. After the interview the Ambassador, General Kaminin and the strong arm men had a long huddle with Gagarin before he was filmed for an ITN interview. Rogov said to Fox, 'Ah well, we all have to compromise!' Fox replied sharply, 'What do you mean! We didn't.'

FATHER AGNELLUS ANDREW

Broadcasts from Rome

My first working meeting with Richard Dimbleby was in the Church of St Denis in Paris during the first Anglo-French TV Week in July 1952. I arrived on a Saturday afternoon to find Richard walking round, note-book in hand, contemplating the tombs of the Kings of France and soaking in the atmosphere of this ancient church full of memories of Joan of Arc. He had arrived the previous day, with all the textbook facts of the place completely mastered and neatly set out on his little cards. Now he was gaining what only the place itself could give so that he would come to his commentator's task the following day clothed with a sense of place and occasion.

Then, as on many later occasions, I had a double job. I worked with Richard all through his preparations and sat beside him during his commentary in the role of expert adviser; and then, when Richard had finished his descriptive commentary and had set the scene, I took over the job as commentator for the religious ceremony itself. I don't know which of these two jobs was the more daunting – to pick up the commentary from where the master himself had left off, or to attempt to satisfy his demand for meticulously accurate and detailed information about every aspect of the event which he was to describe.

In Rome it was: 'Agnellus, who are the Busselanti? Why do they wear that curious crimson damask uniform? What are they in real life? How did they begin? How were these recruited?' and so on, until every fact

*Pope John XXIII with
Archbishop Dante*

was mastered. I think we each of us could have described St Peter's
and the great Piazza outside, blindfold. He loved the enormous
pillared colonnade of Bernini, 'like two arms outstretched to embrace
the world', he said. And he came to know all the folklore of the place,
and the little bits of gossip and delicious minor scandals as well.

He was too English ever quite to understand and accept the Italian
way of ceremonial, with the Masters of Ceremonies giving frank and
open direction as they led Pope and Cardinals through the maze of
elaborate, ancient rites. 'I wish that fellow would stop pushing the old
man around', he said, as Archbishop Dante tried to bring some discipline into Pope John's slightly carefree ritual endeavours. On the other
hand, he very much disliked any attempt to bring the old liturgy up to
date. 'The thing itself speaks,' he said, when we were discussing the
abandonment of Latin and the use of the vernacular, 'you don't need to
understand every single word.' And then he turned to me and said, 'I'm
not going to use your lovely Latin name any more. I am going to call you
"Papa Lamb" ' – and Papa Lamb I was.

Others have written much about his industry and high professionalism. I remember we were in Rome for the Coronation of Pope John
XXIII. Handouts and official papers were late in arriving through some
misunderstanding. In the end, we had to go off with Charles Ricono
of the BBC's European Service to try to get hold of somebody important
in St Peter's late in the afternoon on the day before the event. We found
Archbishop Dell 'Acqua supervising the seating for Cardinals and diplo-
mats in the Basilica. Charles explained our difficulty and persuaded the
Archbishop to come into the Vatican and break open the little cupboard
where the papers were kept. We got back to our hotel at 5 o'clock, and

from then until after 11 I slowly made my way with Richard through every detail of his part of the ceremony. Coffee then, and off he went to his room to do some writing. And I had to begin to prepare my commentary from the beginning.

He was a master in the art of working with unknown producers from other television organisations whose style of cutting and mixing the cameras and whose whole method of production were strange to him. Often he would know only the opening and closing sequences: for the rest he had to follow the producer's decisions. He would have no indication of the line of development or of the length of time that a picture might be held, and yet he went along easily and expertly, fitting himself perfectly into the situation and always tying his commentary into what was relevant on the screen.

And he was unflappable. We were doing a twenty-minute contribution to *Panorama* in October 1962 from Rome on the occasion of the opening of the Vatican Council. The programme had to be fed along the Eurovision line to London at 3 o'clock for inclusion in that night's programme and we were working like beavers in St Peter's. Richard had just finished interviewing Cardinal Gilroy of Sydney when, without warning, all the lights suddenly went out. We had reached the lunch-time break and nothing that Paul Fox could say (and he was eloquent) could induce the Italian technicians to stay on the job. Richard was completely cool. In the end, he continued his work and the rest of the programme was televised using the house lights only.

My last evening with Richard was in Rome at the Coronation of the present Pope, Paul VI. It was a blazing June day in 1963. The ceremony was out of doors and Richard had had to spend a good deal of time out in the open with a handkerchief tied round his head, mastering the seating plans and other details of the ceremony. Afterwards, in the cool of the evening, we went off to have a little supper at a trattoria in the

Coronation of Pope Paul VI

With Father Agnellus Andrew

quiet piazza of S. Maria in Trastevere. We sat in the open, opposite the ancient church with its frescoes exquisitely lighted. It seemed a million miles away from the splendid scarlet and gold of the ceremony from which we had come. We sat there for nearly three hours and then, reluctantly, we got up and made our way back to the hotel, walking slowly through the ancient streets and past the cool fountains of Rome.

With David Wheeler

DAVID WHEELER

Travelling with Dimbleby

On human stories Richard was *Panorama*'s best reporter. His interest in people and places was such that he was seldom bored. Years and years of travel, often tedious and uncomfortable, had not blunted his enthusiasm for an interesting journey. He was the romantic Englishman, to whom a journey on the pre-war Orient Express would have been the highest heaven.

One of the pleasures of far-away places was the thought that very few people there would know him. There would be the rare pleasure of walking about the streets and not being recognised. The penalties of having the best-known face and figure in the country were very great. Autograph hunters lurked round every corner. Strangers came up in restaurants when you were having a quiet dinner after a tiring day. They

made you stand up and shake their hand. People in cars did double-takes, then leaned out of windows and waved. Coach-loads of holiday-makers shouted 'Yoo-hoo – good old Richard!' It was tedious when it happened but, he would ruefully admit, worrying if it didn't.

Thus in Paris, but never in London, he could occasionally indulge in a visit to the night clubs. But he was always faintly apprehensive of being spotted by some English tourist who would raise a loud, shocked cry of 'Good heavens – it's Dimbleby – here!'

The places where he could escape the consequences of fame grew steadily fewer. In the fifties he could go to New York and not be recognised. By 1965, the anonymity had been partly torn aside, thanks to Telstar and Early Bird. His face was familiar to millions of Americans. In Montreal, not a city where you would have expected him to be widely known, I walked with him along the main shopping street to murmurs of 'Isn't that Richard Dimbleby?'

Of course, it was his shape that made him instantly identifiable – the familiar rotundity of a man who was yet surprisingly light and nippy on his feet. His feelings about his shape were ambivalent. He accepted it as part of his public personality – 'my trade-mark' – but from time to time made strenuous efforts to diminish it. These were not completely successful. Away from home, in restaurants in Europe and North America, one watched the complex and losing inner struggle that took place whenever the waiter offered a particularly delicious (but definitely non-slimming) gateau or creamy concoction.

As a thorough-going romantic, he had a passion for casinos. I don't believe he ever won or lost what real gamblers would call real money. It was the atmosphere that drew him. Any itinerary which took him to the Mediterranean would be carefully examined to see if it offered the possibility of a quick diversion to Monte Carlo. Frequently it did.

One recent New Year's Eve found us in Beirut. The Lebanese capital now has a splendid casino, some way out of town. After dinner I was persuaded to take a taxi out with him, sit through a glittering cabaret and then accompany him to the business end of the casino. After a losing streak, he won enough to pay for the entire evening's entertainment and still show a pleasant profit. It was a proud moment. We got back to our hotel at 3 a.m., two hours before an early call to fly to Jordan for the Pope's visit to Jerusalem.

In Jerusalem we met an old friend of his and the programme, King Hussein. The King has appeared many times on *Panorama*. Once, at the height of a Middle East crisis, he was telephoned in Amman by the *Panorama* studio in London. The King himself came on the line with a ringing, 'Hullo, Richard!' Now, in Jerusalem, he shouted, 'Richard! How wonderful to see you here!' and escorted us to a superb lunch of Arab food.

It was inevitably 'Richard' wherever he went, to kings and commoners. In New York, a couple of tough Manhattan cops, driving us around town for a film story on crime, may have started out wondering if the plump Englishman on the back seat of their squad car wasn't some kind of stuffed-shirt and so moderated their language accordingly. Within an hour or so, 'Dicks' and 'Daves' were flowing freely and the air

King Hussein visits Panorama: Sir Ian Jacob (Director-General), Leonard Miall (Head of Television Talks), King Hussein, Abdul Monen Rifai (Jordanian Chief of National Guidance), [now Sir] Gerald Beadle (Director of Television), 20 April 1959

inside the car was blue with the sort of story television vigilantes have nightmares about. U.S. and U.K. had formed a special relationship.

He had many stories to tell, as befitted a man to whom so much had happened. There was the bizarre experience of the servant at his house who one evening went berserk and chased him with a carving knife. Richard finally knocked the man out, with a straight right to the chin. 'Of course, he had to go. I saw him again months later. My car was stopped in a traffic jam, not far from Whitehall, and I caught sight of him, on foot. He saw me and came across. He seemed in good form and quite well turned out. I asked him what he was doing now and he said, "I've got quite a good job, sir. I'm a messenger with the War Office." I looked down at his briefcase and there it was, OHMS. He was carrying official secrets all over London.'

Unnerving experiences on the air figured largely. There was the outside broadcast from the shopping streets of Paris with a French television unit. In the full flow of a live commentary, he realised the point had been reached where he should be seen in vision, walking up the street. But there was no camera for him to talk to.

'There wasn't a single camera in sight – until suddenly one shot round the corner. It was being pushed along by a horde of shouting, gesticulating Frenchmen. It went right *past* me at a rate of knots and disappeared into the distance. As it went by the cameraman screamed at me, "Ils sont fous, monsieur! Complètement fous!"'

He hated incompetent and amateurish producers but remembered with affection another outside broadcast. This came from a London food factory. During rehearsal, the producer had got himself into a complicated tangle with his cameras. To resolve it, he created an artificial corridor by draping a long curtain behind the area where most of the action in the programme was to take place. This, he hoped, would enable him to move his cameras up and down, from one end of the factory to the other, without being seen in vision.

'All went well on the air, until I heard him say, "Camera One, move across *now*." A second or so later, "Camera Two, on your way *now*."

'Unfortunately he'd forgotten they were moving from opposite directions. They tore along behind the drape. They met head-on. The most almighty crash you ever heard!'

The commentator carried on. He always did. His massive reassurance communicated itself off the screen almost as much as on. During a flight to Athens, on his way to interview the Greek King and Queen in Corfu, his aircraft ran into tremendous turbulence. There was a crack that sounded rather like the end of the world. The plane began to heave all over the sky. After a little while the captain said they would be turning back to London.

Among the passengers was a group of Greek Orthodox priests. They looked, according to another member of the *Panorama* party, very anxious indeed. The men of God sweated for some minutes. Then one of them, recognising him, said, 'Ah, Meester Deemblebee! *Please* tell us it will be all right.'

With King Paul and Queen Frederika of Greece, Corfu, July 1963

There was one memorable occasion when Dimbleby was late for a programme. It was the Royal Performance from Bertram Mills's Circus at Olympia and, though Dimbleby sprinted, he missed the start of transmission. Derek Burrell-Davis was the outside broadcast producer:

DEREK BURRELL-DAVIS

Roll up, Roll up!

Typically, it was his professionalism and kindheartedness which caused him momentarily to forget the clock. There were only a few minutes to go when he left his commentary position at the ringside, and crossed the funfair to make a final and personal check on the identities of the party which waited to be presented to the Queen. There also was Coco, clutching a bouquet, shaking with nerves. For years the elegant white-faced clown, Percy Huxter, had received Royalty. But Percy had retired, and Nicolai Poliakoff, despite his smiling make-up as Coco, was almost ready to abdicate from his role of Prince of the Circus, and the honour which was now his.

Richard took him aside to a small room; cajoled, instructed and soothed him. Suddenly, conscious of the time, he fled, skirted the astonished VIPs at a smart pace, and took the shortest way back to his waiting microphone – down the 100-yards long red carpet.

In the television control room we saw it all on camera as our vanished commentator made his welcome reappearance, and swept with dignity, yet at speed, between the two lines of celebrities and performers. I concluded a protracted opening camera sequence as he came up on his microphone to introduce a gala circus performance in aid of the Imperial Cancer Research Fund.

128

Unknown to viewers and to most of his colleagues, from 1960 for over five years Richard Dimbleby lived with cancer. His doctors and family helped the 'Daily Mail' to reconstruct those five years to show how living with cancer need not be impossible:

JULIAN HOLLAND

The Story of Dimbleby's Cancer

It was early in 1960 when Richard Dimbleby first noticed he had a swelling. It wasn't much and it wasn't painful and he was a busy man.

Monday was a fourteen-hour day working on *Panorama*. Tuesday was spent at Richmond with his newspapers until the evening, when he did a *Twenty Questions* broadcast. Wednesday was spent working at home. Thursday and Friday he was at Richmond again, working on his newspapers.

Often he was out all day Saturday on extra jobs. He ran two film companies producing industrial films.

Richard Dimbleby was a very busy man. He ignored the swelling.

But by August 1960 the swelling had increased considerably though it still gave no pain. Dimbleby thought it best to go to his local doctor.

His doctor examined him and was in no doubt what was wrong. As he looked out of the window, wondering how best to break the news, Dimbleby said to him: 'You needn't tell me what it is. I know.'

Richard Dimbleby's family and his doctors have made available the history of his case to help combat the general fear and ignorance of the disease. Many doctors believe the fight against cancer is being frustrated by the public's treatment of it as a 'taboo' subject.

This is the story of five salvaged years; of what a man can achieve despite the disease; of how fear, even in a very bad case, can be overcome.

Richard Dimbleby went into St Thomas's Hospital, London, on 15 August 1960, and was operated on the following day. The chances in favour of a complete cure at that moment were four to one – provided the original growth had not started to spread.

After the surgeon had removed the lump Dimbleby was examined carefully. He was a big man – 18 st. 7 lb. at the time – and the urologist on the case, Mr Ronald Robinson, found it difficult to feel anything under the fat of the abdomen.

But, under an anaesthetic, a mass was felt to the right side of his abdomen. The original cancer *had* already spread along the lymphatic glands to a new site.

The doctors decided to tackle the secondary growth with a five-week course of radiotherapy. The course of treatment began on 1 September at St Thomas's, under Dr Ian Churchill-Davidson. Massive destructive doses of X-rays were directed at Dimbleby's abdomen five times a week.

Five days after the treatment began Richard Dimbleby was on television to introduce a new series of *Panorama*. The following day he was on the radio, chairing *Twenty Questions*.

The affected glands shrank. On 3 October Dimbleby went in for his

*Leaving hospital for
Twenty Questions after
first operation for cancer,
23 August 1960*

last dose of radio-therapy treatment after appearing on that night's
edition of *Panorama*. The second round in the battle seemed to have
been won.

By this time the disease had become Dimbleby's special subject. He
was learning all he could about it. He arranged to see demonstrations of
the machines used in treatment. He listened to all the theories about
what caused cancer and discussed cancer research in detail.

His interest was insatiable. After the final treatment Dimbleby went
off for a drink with a few of the hospital staff – it had become a custom
and they went either to the local pub or the staff canteen – to talk some
more about cancer.

The next day he was back at work at the newspapers in Richmond and
he remained well and fit in every respect for the next nineteen months.

From time to time Dimbleby revisited St Thomas's for detailed
examinations – all aimed at detecting the first signs of any new growths.

He was able to work at his normal pace. In early November 1960 he
went to America for *Panorama*, came back in time for the Festival of
Remembrance Service and the Cenotaph outside broadcast for television; in December he covered the royal wedding in Brussels; in April

1961 he went to Moscow; in May he went to Rome and Naples to cover the Queen's visit.

It was on 2 May 1962 that Dimbleby complained of a dull ache in the upper reaches of the back. He went into St Thomas's, where the radiographs revealed that the glands were enlarged alongside the vertebrae and in the structure that stands between the lungs.

Another course of radiotherapy began. On 2 May and 5 May both areas were given radiotherapy treatment. On 7 May Dimbleby was on television as usual introducing *Panorama*. On 9 May he was back for another dose of radiation.

Once again the glands that appeared to be affected by cancer reverted to their former size.

The pattern of Dimbleby's life continued uninterrupted. Before the end of the month he was in Sweden for a special edition of *Panorama*. He covered the Trooping the Colour ceremony, the Middlesbrough by-election, the first Telstar broadcast, King Olav's visit to Scotland and the funeral of Queen Wilhelmina. For nine whole months he remained free of trouble.

However, in March 1963 Dimbleby began to have pain in the lower portion of the back when he was standing a lot. X-rays showed growths in the second and third lumbar (loin) vertebrae, and a further abdominal examination under a general anaesthetic on 14 March showed a recurrence of the enlargement of the glands in the earlier site in the belly.

Between 15 March and 29 March the abdomen was treated with radiotherapy, though the treatment did not prevent Dimbleby appearing as usual in his chair in *Panorama*.

During this period of treatment Dimbleby was given a general anaesthetic each time to reduce the risk of radiation sickness which might have resulted from the concentrated dose of radiation.

It was usual for Dimbleby to have his radiotherapy treatment on Friday evenings whenever possible. This gave him the weekend to rest in – radiotherapy treatment may have a temporary weakening effect on some patients – before Monday's exhausting day on *Panorama*.

He had by now become adept at his own diagnosis. When he felt a pain he was always able to work out how the cancer had travelled from the last known site to attack the new area. Each time the doctors only confirmed his own diagnosis.

In this way, by taking a deep interest in what was happening to him, Dimbleby was coming to terms with his illness.

Dimbleby had already undergone two of the main types of treatment for cancer – radiotherapy and surgery. The third main method – hormone treatment – is mostly used in treating cancer of the breast. All these forms of treatment have advanced substantially in the past decade.

Surgery: If the growth is visible, accessible and reasonably circumscribed, it can be cut out. The great forward strides in the techniques of surgery and the use of antibiotics, transfusions and better anaesthetics have made success possible in operations that could not be attempted ten years ago.

Radiation: Certain forms of radiation cause cancer, making groups of body cells behave in the erratic way that is the characteristic of cancer.

But massive doses of radiation destroy the imbalanced cells, curing the cancerous growth.

Many of the enormous machines now used in radiography rotate about the patient so that the target is always being hit from a different angle, in order to spare the skin and healthy tissues in the track of the beam. The patient feels nothing during treatment, needs only to rest for a while afterwards.

By the time of the third spell of treatment Dimbleby had been living with a particularly virulent form of cancer for three years. According to the mythology of cancer he should have been dead long before or, at least, in great agony.

In fact, at this stage, it was still possible Dimbleby might be completely cured.

Radiation and surgery techniques have developed to the point where much pain can be relieved, even when growths are too widespread or advanced to be cured. When enlarged glands, for instance, start pressing on sensory nerves, they can be irradiated sufficiently to dispel pain if not to cure.

From March 1963 until January 1965 Dimbleby had no sign that he was not free of the disease.

He went about his business with great vigour. In that period he covered Princess Alexandra's wedding, the State visit of the King of the Belgians, the lying-in-state of Pope John, President Kennedy's visit to Germany, the Coronation of Pope Paul, the State visit of the King of Greece, the service at Westminster Abbey for the death of President Kennedy, the Pope's visit to Israel, special editions of *Panorama* from Paris and Germany, from Canada and Luxembourg, the opening of the Forth Bridge, the American election.

But in January 1965 Dimbleby began to get pains in the lower part of his back and numbness in his right flank. Radiographs showed that the eleventh and twelfth dorsal vertebrae had collapsed through destruction by secondary growths.

Between 15 January and 9 February he was given three sessions of radiotherapy, which relieved the pain. Also between 15 January and 9 February he appeared each Monday on *Panorama*, covered Churchill's lying-in-state and the State funeral, and appeared in a number of programmes of reminiscences about Churchill.

Despite Dimbleby's refusal to give in or to ease the pressure of his work through the next six months, this period was in fact the beginning of the end. The occurrence of growths was beginning to accelerate. Further secondaries were found in his diaphragm, his back and ribs.

Yet, an incident in the summer of 1965 shows that even at that late stage Dimbleby found the disease neither physically intolerable nor nerve-racking. He went off on his summer holiday feeling, as he said, 'as fit as a fiddle'.

The Dimbleby family together with Churchill-Davidson, now a close friend, went boating in Devon.

One day off Dartmouth they ran into a nasty storm. It was a fearful moment – for the doctor.

Churchill-Davidson had already warned Dimbleby to be careful of falling while his spine was still in a weak condition. A fall could have meant instant paralysis.

David Dimbleby turned the boat into the 8 ft waves to avoid being swamped, but it was lifting sickeningly over them, then slapping hard down into the troughs between them. Richard Dimbleby stood in the wheelhouse, holding the rail, riding the waves on his tiptoes. And behind him, Churchill-Davidson's face turned white.

As the boat lifted up and down, Dimbleby nudged his son, indicated the anxious doctor and winked.

When they got into harbour Dimbleby apologised to Churchill-Davidson for the rough ride he'd been given and said he was sorry if he'd been made seasick.

'I wasn't sick,' replied Churchill-Davidson, 'I was just worried about you. But if your back can stand *that* it can stand anything. I shouldn't worry about falling any more.'

Mrs Wyndham Goldie was my redoubtable deputy throughout the period I was in charge of the talks and current affairs programmes on BBC Television. I asked her to take a special responsibility for the General Election Results programmes, for the transmogrification of Panorama, and for launching the first programmes giving consumer advice on named products, all enterprises in which she collaborated closely with Richard Dimbleby. She recalled his courage in an article written for the 'Sunday Telegraph':

GRACE WYNDHAM GOLDIE

The Start of 'Choice'

Richard Dimbleby never questioned the authority of even the youngest producer. He never quibbled about details of content and would happily accept linking words written for him and make only minor changes. Yet he would never accept a programme which cut across the grain of his personality.

It's the existence of this grain, of this quality inherent in their very being, which makes the great television professionals. It wasn't simply because Ed Murrow was so brilliantly a professional that he dominated the best of American television for so long. Nor was Dimbleby's continuing and almost embarrassing success – so that people asked 'Why must it always be Dimbleby?' – due to his professionalism alone.

There are plenty of television professionals. Some of them seem to have chromium plate in their veins. Not Richard. He existed as a man. He wanted to be a surgeon. And when I got to know him I realised that he combined, with his meticulous attention to detail, a human compassion and yet a professional detachment which made me understand why he regretted that he had to go into the family newspaper business; why so many of his friends were surgeons, and why he had a continuing interest in surgery.

All this, and his personal courage, was brought home to me one night early in 1962 when I was making a pilot for a programme called *Choice* which, for the first time in television, gave advice to consumers, naming manufacturers and prices.

The Federation of British Industries was alarmed. They warned me that there was a serious danger of lawsuits involving sums of money. In the early days eight lawyers had to vet each script and each videotape before transmission. I believed that the only person who could undertake this difficult job was Richard, and he accepted when he was convinced that it was a public service.

But we had to make a pilot programme to persuade the Board of Governors that *Choice* was a starter. The dates for recording the pilot were fixed. Richard said: 'I'm sorry, but they're absolutely impossible and so I can't do the thing at all. Obviously whoever does the later programmes must do the pilot.'

Now I knew then, what we all now know, that Richard was undergoing treatment for cancer and he told me that the reason why he

couldn't manage this particular day was that it was one on which the hospital had arranged for him to have treatment. I said that we would make any arrangement to suit him and he eventually agreed that if he walked through the programme in the early afternoon, went off at four, and came back at six for a final rehearsal and recording, all would be well. He was always punctual. So I was astonished when 6.30, 7, 7.15 came and there was no sign of Richard.

I was told that it would now be impossible to complete the rehearsal and then record. Just after 7.15 Richard arrived, said 'I'm terribly sorry', and hurried up to the studio. We rehearsed in part, then he recorded brilliantly a half-rehearsed programme. When I went downstairs I found him eating and drinking and amusing the rest of the participants by some of the good-humoured stories he told so well. Then he took me aside and said: 'I'm so sorry if I messed up the pilot, they didn't warn me that I was going to be under a total anaesthetic for two hours and I'd no idea what was happening.'

That he should have carried on with this difficult rehearsal and recording was astonishing. That he should under these circumstances apologise for being late was incredible. But that was Richard. It was impossible not to admire him as well as to like him. It was equally impossible to imagine him ever being petty or mean or ungenerous. And this came over the television screen and gave authority not only to his own performance but to the programmes in which he appeared.

135

PAUL FOX

Above: Telstar, London

Via Telstar and Return

New York's International Airport was its usual bustling self. As the lines of passengers shuffled past the shirtsleeved customs officers, one of the red-capped porters ambled across: 'Aren't you Mr Dimbleby?'

In London that question, usually preceded by a slow stare, would have been familiar enough. In Berlin, in Rome, even in Paris, it would not have been out of the ordinary. But this was New York – and when Richard Dimbleby arrived there one July evening in 1962, even Americans turned to stare.

The reason for their new-found familiarity with the face known to all in Britain lay in a ball-shaped piece of metal hurtling through the sky: Telstar, the first communication satellite to provide a live television link between Europe and North America. The night before his arrival in New York, Richard had notched up another first: the first man to have televised live from Europe to America.

On 23 July 1962 Richard spoke from Brussels on behalf of sixteen countries when he welcomed American audiences to their first live television view of Europe across 3,000 miles of Atlantic Ocean. Now he was back for the return half – and another first: the first Englishman to televise live from America to Britain. And to make him feel at home, the *New York Times* said of him on the morning of his arrival: 'He dominates Britain's television in a way that has no equivalent in the United States.'

That one historic broadcast from Europe – that cheerful 'Hullo, New York' from Brussels – made Richard Dimbleby's friendly face and ample figure almost as familiar in the United States as in the United Kingdom. Within twenty-four hours of his arrival he had appeared on CBS with Walter Cronkite and also on NBC Television. New York's press corps waited upon him. *Variety* – that bible of American show-business – spread his story across three columns. And as he stood on 53rd Street, in the shadow of Rockefeller Center, getting ready to televise live to London, many an American passer-by knew exactly who he was.

But they couldn't have known that the first New York-based telecast was nearly swept off the screens. At the rehearsal, everything had gone smoothly. The cameras on the roof of the Rockefeller Center had pierced through the haze to give us perfect pictures of the towering Manhattan skyline. The camera in the Sixth Avenue drug store had just the right shot. A smooth and speedy commentary setting the scene was needed now; we only had ten minutes available; after that, we would lose the satellite. So there was a double nervous strain: the importance of the occasion with the twitching uncertainty whether the picture would successfully bounce off the moving satellite to England, and the urgent need to contain the programme within that limited span of time as soon as London signalled it was able to see New York.

With less than a minute to go, Richard's monitor – the television set that would show him which picture was going out – collapsed. There he was, in mid-town Manhattan, the first Briton to televise live across the Atlantic, and he could not himself see any of the pictures that were being transmitted. Once again he was, for all practical purposes, blind. He could not see whether the pictures the American director was selecting were of the New York skyline or the cops or the drug store or the sidewalk. He had to guess and hope that the transmission would follow the rehearsal.

It did, fortunately. And after five hazardous minutes, the picture came back on Richard's monitor. The trouble was over, though I doubt whether anyone at home ever noticed that something had gone very wrong, for Richard spoke as confidently as ever. But in those five minutes the American television crew learned and understood why he was the master of the craft of television reporting.

Telstar, New York, with Walter Cronkite

LEONARD MIALL

A Bouncing Ball to Comfort a Distracted Child

Richard Dimbleby always gave generously of his time and skill to broadcast appeals on behalf of causes near to his heart. Altogether he raised nearly £1 million. He was particularly concerned, and particularly effective, when the object of the appeal was relief of human suffering from some sudden emergency. One of these was the earthquake disaster in Western Persia in the late summer of 1962. Dimbleby appeared on the screen at the end of the news on Wednesday 5 September and showed pictures of the appalling damage done by the biggest natural disaster that had happened in any country for years. He said, 'The need is enormous and the need is terribly urgent. It's got to be something in the next forty-eight hours to be really effective. Not only for the drugs, the splints for shattered legs, for the blood plasma, for all the other necessities, but for something like this' *and at that point he held up what the Red Cross call a 'Disaster Bag' and showed that it had things like a toothbrush and towel, a handkerchief, a mug, a ball of string, pins, a spoon, a pencil and something else.*'Because children, thank goodness, are the quickest people to disassociate themselves from the horrors around them, if they have got something to do, however simple it is, every one of these Disaster Bags has in it a ball – an ordinary ball that a child can play with and which will take its mind off things.' *He ended,* 'I believe that you will want to help. This is the quickest, best and most effective way to do it. I have never asked for anything more seriously than I am for this, at this moment.'

138

Dimbleby's viewers did respond and respond quickly. £407,000 came in.

A year later there was again an appalling earthquake tragedy, this time at Skopje, the capital of Yugoslav Macedonia. Again Dimbleby was asked to make an emergency television appeal. He agreed to do so the same night, but then refused to go on the air until the Foreign Office were prepared to announce that in addition to the help the British Government was giving to Yugoslavia they would provide aircraft to deliver the goods that might be purchased out of private donations. Richard spoke movingly about the desperate need for shelter and the material for prefabricated houses. He said on 1 August 1963, 'The Foreign Office have agreed to find the planes if we can find the money, and I am wondering if among the 10 million or so of you who are watching, we can find this amount of money now. The planes are due to leave on August 2nd or 3rd in time to assemble these buildings and provide shelter for these 100,000 homeless.' *He ended:* 'I do hope, as you did for the Persian earthquake last year, that you will respond in helping these desperately unhappy and stricken people.'

Again the response was immediate and overwhelming. The original target was £100,000. Within a week it had passed £250,000. The total was again over £400,000. The BBC had used its own prestige and that of Richard Dimbleby to challenge the public to respond in a time limit and the response had been magnificent. Dimbleby was convinced that the viewers were owed a report on the use to which the money had been put. With David J. Webster as producer, and a camera team, he went to see Skopje for himself and for Panorama's viewers:

DAVID J. WEBSTER

The Tragedy of Skopje

'The real tragedy of Skopje hits you and hits you very hard when you come to this cemetery on the side of the hill just outside the city. Particularly when you come on a day like this with low cloud in the sky and driving rain blowing across everything. Because this is where they brought eleven hundred men, women and children and a lot of tiny babies and buried them all in these trenches, giving each one a simple spade-shaped red headboard.'

It was with these words that Richard opened the film that we made together in the aftermath of the Skopje earthquake of August 1963 as he walked slowly through the fresh graves on the side of a Macedonian hill. This was a very different Richard from the urbane figure to whom we had become accustomed as he presided over State occasions. At Skopje he found again his old role as a brilliant reporter covering a story of misery and suffering with distinction and with feeling.

In Skopje more than eleven hundred people had died and 80 per cent of the city had been destroyed. Those who were left were threatened with floods. The four members of the *Panorama* team were sharing a tent provided by one of the relief organisations. There was a lot of water in it and like the rest of the town we were in danger of being swept away. Richard slept at the end nearest the swollen river and it was agreed that if he sailed past us during the night we would all take it as a signal to leave.

He was not well, his back troubled him, but he remained totally professional and unflustered. He was the only one of the team who had enough common sense to bring not only brandy and instant coffee but a tiny stove on which throughout our stay he brewed the mixture and provided us all with our breakfast.

To many people Richard Dimbleby seemed to represent authority and officialdom. They would not have got that impression in Skopje. His overwhelming feeling was to break through the bureaucracy and the petty barriers which stood between the Macedonians and the relief of their suffering.

Richard did his best reporting when he was dealing with ordinary people. The solidity of his personality and his authority were an effective counterpoint to the sad and chaotic. He mediated between the suffering of this remote land and the concern of a more comfortable Britain. One of his strongest characteristics was that of reassurance. There are many stories in which you just don't want reassurance, but at Skopje it was this which gave his work a special quality. Standing in ruin he seemed an emissary from a more ordered and rational world who would see that something was done to help, and done soon.

With David J. Webster at Skopje

Barto Stuart was in charge of the young British volunteer engineers and specialists who were helping rehouse the thousands of Skopje's homeless. He recalls:

When I brought Richard and his *Panorama* team from the wrecked railway station to my Headquarters tent we found the entire humble establishment awash after heavy rainstorms. There was Richard in gum-boots and candlelight, wading in water almost up to his knees, with spanner and screwdriver cheerfully engaged in making up his ex-Army bunk for the night. His arrival in the midst of a terrible human tragedy brought a ray of sorely lacking common sense and sanity. I still see him, cigar in mouth, and feet in water, brewing coffee on his tiny camping stove, one cup at a time, for everyone present. His terrific humour and charm made us all forget – for a few hours at least – the tragedy outside, our own anxieties and the chilly damp cold everywhere around us. He was not an awe-inspiring figure but a dear friend and father, and a very accessible giant among men.

When he left after an all too short five-day stay he managed to secure a compartment for his team and equipment. He placed himself at the carriage window which happened to be shaped like a TV screen. Quickly realising its potential, he began an unforgettable 10-minute miming act. As the train finally departed Richard still stood framed in his screen, making the craziest faces, and his newly made friends and

admirers had tears of non-stop laughter and affection running down their cheeks. We had witnessed a performance which I still consider on a par with the best mimes of Charlie Chaplin or Norman Wisdom.

Immediately on return he spent a whole day telephoning wives and mothers of all my volunteers at Skopje giving messages and telling them of the work we were doing. What he did not add was that without himself and his appeal there would never have been any British relief work at Skopje.

Richard Dimbleby's Broadcast Appeals

		£	s.	d.
May 1948	Royal Alfred Aged Merchant Seamen's Institution	1,674	13	3
September 1949	Missions to Seamen	3,024	6	2
December 1950	Salvation Army	3,018	1	3
May 1951 (London Region only)	Hostels for Crippled and Invalid Women Workers	862	15	0
January 1952	Missions to Seamen	2,579	11	6
March 1953	Church of England Children's Society	1,701	16	11
February 1954	Royal National Life Boat Institution	3,304	2	5
February 1956 (London Region only)	House of St Barnabas in Soho	911	7	2
October 1956	Missions to Seamen	3,016	0	11
January 1958	Training Ship *Foudroyant*	772	0	0
February 1959 (TV)	National Marriage Guidance Council	1,080	7	1
August 1959	Missions to Seamen	2,733	1	11
March 1960	National Society for Mentally Handicapped Children	1,956	0	0
July 1961	Oxford Committee for Famine Relief	105,941	3	8
September 1962 (TV)	Persian Earthquake Relief	407,000	0	0
June 1963 (TV)	Red Cross Centenary Appeal	2,131	7	4
August 1963 (TV)	Skopje Earthquake Relief (War on Want)	402,000	0	0
December 1963	British Wireless for the Blind	37,825	0	0
July 1965 (TV)	Enterprise Neptune of the National Trust	3,800	0	0
	Total	£985,331	14	7

One of the most tragically sudden outside broadcasts for which Richard had the minimum time to prepare was the state funeral of President Kennedy on 25 November 1963. That night he introduced Panorama via Telstar from Washington with simple and moving words as he described the sorrowing scenes:

RICHARD DIMBLEBY

President Kennedy's Funeral

The two children join their mother, little Caroline and little John, such poignant figures. And everybody about them in black, and they in their best coats of another colour. . . .

President Lyndon Johnson has just arrived there. On his right-hand side is the Head of the American Secret Service, and above them the tall and splendid figure, in his robes and his mitre, of Cardinal Cushing. With him, Archbishop O'Boyle, and other members of the Roman Catholic Church here, to receive, with an arm about her shoulders, Mrs Kennedy, and give his hand to the two little children. . . .

All the time Mrs Kennedy preserves this quiet silent dignity. Many people ask how much longer she can continue. And the family follow behind. The President, his face lined with sorrow and indeed with strain which he has shown in the three days since he took office, follows slowly behind into his place. . . .

Those invited to attend the Mass are waiting in this, like all the Roman Catholic churches, highly decorated in a multitude of marbles and colours. President de Gaulle follows up the steep steps, Queen Frederika, King Baudouin, the Chancellor of Austria, the President and the Chancellor of West Germany – two by two – they enter from the brilliant sunshine, through the West door of the Cathedral, and inside to where the Low Pontifical Requiem begins, the choir chanting as they come in. . . .

And thus, here in the United States, the official events of a sad and bitter day have come to an end. They leave behind, burning like the eternal flame that lit his graveside an hour ago, a thousand memories of the man lost to this nation and to the world. . . .

If there is one thing of which every American citizen is quite certain, it is that he will never forget this day.

The Director of Television worked with Dimbleby for nearly thirty years. In the spring of 1965 he analysed the reasons for Dimbleby's long-lasting success as a commentator:

KENNETH ADAM

Master of Associate Material

Given a natural quickness of mind and a reasonable command of the language, most broadcasters who have to undertake a spontaneous commentary will rely on these talents to get them through almost any occasion. Not so Dimbleby. Though the measure of his gift in both respects is greater than anyone's I know, it is not enough for him. He is the master of 'associate material', which he absorbs prodigiously and produces aptly, weaving it in and out of his narrative with the greatest of ease – or apparent ease. Travel with him in an aircraft to an overseas assignment, and you will find him surrounded by books bearing on the next broadcast (not the next but one) which he reads with great speed but without noting very much down. He has a remarkable memory which takes in temporarily and then rejects after the performance. It is like an athlete's capacity for producing a final burst, or the last few inches of levitation.

He has sometimes been criticised for his attitude towards 'the Establishment'. This springs from a natural respect for order and tradition, not from a mindless conservatism. He is a man much moved by cruelty and intolerance and does not pretend to be impartial towards

Linking television cameras of ten European countries, 2 June 1959

such things. In addition to his broadcasting, he is a newspaper proprietor, a farmer, and a very happy and fortunate husband and father.

Though his face, grave or gay, and ample figure are a household
picture, he is probably at his best (and satellite programmes have recently
brought him American reviews which indisputably put him among the
world's best) when commentating, *off* screen, on great occasions, a
Churchill funeral, a royal wedding, a Pope's inauguration. Sitting in a
central control room, faced with a battery of monitors, fitting his words
to the changing pattern of pictures as chosen by the producer, he is an
imperturbable master of his craft, and never more reliably so than
when things happen unexpectedly or when things do not happen at all.

*Few knew these qualities more intimately than Antony Craxton, who
produced more than a hundred major outside broadcasts with Richard
Dimbleby, and was his ally in countless battles with the authorities to secure
proper facilities for television to cover public events:*

ANTONY CRAXTON

Commentator at Royal Events

Few people have any conception of the complexities a television commentator faces on a large-scale outside broadcast. One should think it
difficult enough to describe events taking place in sight – which they
very often are not – while at the same time watching the same events on
a television screen. But in addition to this, a commentator has to wear a
pair of headphones, through which he can hear in one earpiece the
sounds of the event – the band, horses' hooves, etc. – and in the other
the producer giving to him and the many cameramen detailed, involved
instructions. Thus, while describing solemn events of a State Funeral,
for instance, the poor commentator will be getting constant interrup-

*Antony Craxton and
Dimbleby briefing Euro-
vision commentators before
Princess Alexandra's
wedding*

tions to his train of thought. He virtually has to have a split mind, which can keep a fluent commentary going while at the same time absorbing information from the producer which will be essential to him as the broadcast proceeds. Moreover, the instructions the producer gives to the cameramen are equally important to the commentator, as they often forewarn him of what pictures are being planned and which he can then be ready to describe.

For Richard Dimbleby, these difficulties were an integral part of the job of commentating, and so supreme a master of his craft was he that never did they prevent him from giving of his best. Very often when I was the producer I got carried away and used to give my own commentary as I switched from picture to picture – a commentary which, of course, Richard could hear all too clearly – putting words into his mouth. This must have caused him embarrassment on occasions, as he often pulled my leg about it, but at no time in the countless outside broadcasts we undertook together did he lose control of himself, and there were many occasions when the conditions under which he worked would have daunted the brave. Snow, torrential rain, suffocating heat, Richard suffered them all with a philosophical outlook which made him the great professional he was.

One occasion which challenged even Richard's powers was the departure of Princess Margaret and Lord Snowdon on their honeymoon on 6 May 1960. Richard and I had left Westminster Abbey almost immediately after the marriage service had finished, to journey to the Tower of London, from where the Royal Yacht *Britannia* was sailing. We had decided to go on the air as the Royal couple left Buckingham Palace, and to fill the twenty minutes the journey to the Tower was expected to take with a planned sequence of pictures from the four Tower cameras. Little did we think that the twenty minutes would be more than doubled before the car arrived. Having completed our rehearsed sequence, we searched for visual material to interest the viewers while they waited: the Tower itself, the Bridge, the jetty, the Yeomen

Warders, the *Britannia* of course, the launch, the skyline of London; every possibility was used. The most remarkable aspect of this unexpected marathon was that Richard wove his commentary into a masterpiece of continuity, so that few people realised that what was being seen and said had not been planned in great detail beforehand. Unrelated subjects and objects were somehow, by Richard's description, made into a pattern that at once seemed natural and flowing. Towards the end, after the marathon had been in progress some fifty minutes, Richard did show some impatience towards the three or four helicopters circling noisily overhead, and which must have seriously disturbed his concentration, seated in the open as he was. He confessed to me afterwards that he had exhausted his almost inexhaustible fund of information about the scene, and was ready to break into silence at any moment.

I also vividly recall the opening of the Wedding broadcast. Richard had forgotten that instead of beginning, as originally planned, at ten o'clock, we had decided, for technical reasons, to start five minutes earlier. He was due to open our transmission, in vision, on the lawn outside the North Door of the Abbey. Two minutes before time I noticed that he wasn't at this camera position, and asked where he was. I was extremely alarmed to hear from a cameraman in the Abbey that he was strolling quietly down the Choir checking seating arrangements, oblivious of the urgency of his presence outside. The only way to get him to the start on time was for the cameraman to startle the distinguished assembled company by calling out to Richard from his lofty position in the Abbey and indicating the need for some haste. Richard arrived a few seconds before the broadcast began, and no viewer would have guessed from his opening remarks that he had run the last fifty yards or so.

Some years earlier I remember an occasion when the usually meticulous Royal arrangements went wrong and caused us acute embarrassment. It was the unveiling by Her Majesty the Queen of the Merchant Navy Memorial at Tower Hill in November 1955. The Memorial is sunk below ground level and consists of a central area with two small side alcoves. In order to get a television camera into one of these wings we had buried a cable at an early stage of construction so it would not look unsightly on the day. As the photograph shows, the camera, on a movable four-wheeled truck, was tucked away in the wing, together with the choir, and almost completely filled the area. The Queen, on her inspection of the Memorial, was due to walk across the front of this alcove, but to our consternation the architect escorted her into it to one side of the choir, and thus out of sight of our cameras. We knew that it would be virtually impossible for Her Majesty to walk right round the alcove as our camera would block her progress. All we could do was to move the camera forward on to the grass, knocking over military band music stands in the process, and subsequently to heave on the submerged cable and, in so doing, lift the flagstones, in an effort to allow the Queen room to squeeze through. My panic-stricken instructions to the cameramen, all of which Richard could hear only too well, did not prevent him from calmly describing the scene, well aware of the predicament we were in. He conveyed nothing of this to the viewing public.

Merchant Navy Memorial
(TV camera to right of band)

At Princess Alexandra's wedding on 24 April 1963, instead of using a number of different commentators, which was customary when our cameras were ranged over a wide area, I decided to break new ground and use Richard alone. He was in a sound-proof box in our central control room at the Abbey, immediately behind my position overlooking all the twenty or so monitor screens. The advantages were enormous. Richard could see, as I could, exactly when events were about to happen at Kensington Palace, Clarence House, or Buckingham Palace, as well as along the route and inside and outside the Abbey. This meant that he could work far more closely with me. For instance, I could tell him over his headphones to watch the Kensington Palace picture and that, as soon as Princess Alexandra stepped out from her home, we would switch to those cameras immediately. While describing events elsewhere he was able to keep an eye on that vital screen. Even before I switched to Kensington Palace, Richard had said 'and as Queen Elizabeth the Queen Mother arrives at the Abbey, some three or four miles away the bride leaves her home for the last time', or words to that effect. Again, when we picked up the bridegroom's car as it sped along the route, Richard was able to follow it continuously, even though we were only showing its progress to the viewers from time to time. Consequently, he knew its exact position whenever I decided to switch to it. This method of describing events can only be of value if many locations are involved, and where split-second switching from one to the other is necessary.

Dimbleby's view of Princess Alexandra's wedding

For the historic funeral of Sir Winston Churchill, Richard had two positions in the West Gallery of St Paul's Cathedral, and our control room was in the Crypt. From one box Richard described the entire procession from Westminster to Waterloo; from the other, overlooking the Nave, he described the Service below him.

This was a mammoth effort for him. Five hours as sole commentator, then no relaxation – a hurried journey to Television Centre to edit the tapes ready for a two and a half hour transmission that night with a fresh commentary.

Few people can realise the homework Richard undertook for this epic task; the vast amount of reading necessary to assimilate every detail of the solemn events. On this broadcast he achieved a perfection he had never attained before.

As part of his preparation Dimbleby had arranged to meet the Duke of Norfolk, who as Earl Marshal was in charge of the arrangements, at 5 p.m. on the day before the funeral to settle any outstanding questions for his final commentary. The Duke of Norfolk later wrote in 'The Times':

'As it happened we met at 4.15 a.m. in New Palace Yard at the final rehearsal. Dimbleby asked me what I proposed to do and when I told him I was going to move up and down the route he said: "May I tag on with my car?" At about 7.30, as the morning grew lighter, he came up to me on Tower Hill and said: "Unless you want me this evening we can call off our meeting – I have all I want and you will be busy!"

It will be hard to match his gentle kindness, sense of humour, intelligence, and tact.'

Opposite:
The Earl Marshal leading
the gun carriage party

West gallery,
St Paul's Cathedral,
Churchill's funeral,
30 January 1965

The Churchill funeral broadcast will long be remembered by those who saw it and studied by generations to come. Some 600 letters came to the BBC afterwards, of which these are samples:

'It was a triumph for everyone concerned, organisers, cameramen and commentator. I need Richard Dimbleby's flow of language adequately to express my thanks for everything. Perhaps you would thank him, as much for his silences as for his excellent commentary.'

'I watched from 8.30 a.m. until the end and in my humble opinion the BBC – always excellent – excelled itself! My genuine gratitude to all – no matter how humble their parts may have been – who helped to achieve such a wonderful result.'

'I feel I must offer to you and your colleagues grateful thanks for the truly magnificent way in which you showed that epoch-making event, especially at such very short notice. The commentary of Mr Richard Dimbleby was also absolutely splendid, and fully worthy of the solemnity and splendour of the occasion, as was indeed also the carriage and behaviour of the soldiers who had the truly arduous task of carrying for long periods their precious burden. Altogether the whole proceedings were worthy of the wonderful man in whose honour they, in fact, were arranged for, and those of us who witnessed them will never forget.'

Pall bearers the Earl of Avon and Field-Marshal Lord Slim behind Earl Attlee

Richard himself received another 500 requests for the poem by Avril Anderson which he read at the conclusion of his commentary:

RICHARD DIMBLEBY

At Bladon

. . . the village of Bladon, just two miles from Blenheim where the lych-gate of the church and the tower of the church can be seen on a winter's day. It's close by this church and this churchyard that the Spencer-Churchills lie buried. Not in any lordly isolation, but buried with them down there, John Harry Adams, and Percy Merry, and Kathleen Jones, and William Partlitt, and John Abbott, and Arthur Sawyer, and two little unnamed children aged six and seven. The church itself is as simple and unpretentious as are the graves that lie by it. These the graves of the Churchills – this the grave of Winston Churchill. It lies next to the place where his mother, whom he said was to him like the Evening Star, is buried under those plants that grow. This is the cross of the grave of his father, Lord Randolph Churchill. And all this lies within sight of the monumental palace of Blenheim that a grateful Sovereign gave to Winston Churchill's ancestor for his services to England, the huge house where Sir Winston said that he took two important decisions – 'to be born and to marry, and I did not regret either'. Here as a boy he played. As a young man he took the train to Handborough, and a lift on the estate cart up to the Palace. Here he returned in the days of his fame. Here they bring him today to lie forever.

> From the Hall of Kings they bore him then,
> The greatest of all Englishmen,
> To the nation's, the world's, requiem
>   At Bladon.
>
> Drop, English earth, on him beneath,
> To our sons and their sons bequeath
> His glories, and our pride and grief
>   At Bladon.
>
> For lionheart that lies below,
> That feared not toil, nor tears, nor foe,
> Let the oak stand, though tempests blow
>   At Bladon.
>
> So Churchill sleeps; yet surely wakes,
> Old warrior, where the morning breaks
> On sunlit uplands – but the heart aches
>   At Bladon.

That broadcast was recalled a year later in the television column of 'New Christian':

JAMES MITCHELL

The Private Interior Truth

You don't *love* a man because he's a professional: you tend, rather, to distrust him, particularly if his professional expertise is directed towards the projection of an image which sometimes seems too gentle to be true.

But people did love Richard Dimbleby and I for one am not ashamed to acknowledge that I was, and remain, one of them. And since I think the roots of my affection for him have a general significance in terms of the whole medium of television I have decided to explain why.

I think it was because he was a person. Television is a medium which eats people. It builds a man into an image: instant soft and desirable female or instant rugged masculinity, always there for screening and plugging and *satisfying* the aching unconscious needs of the viewer. And if the image goes wrong or the glitter wears a bit thin then the tele-magnates smash the image, drop the idol and start all over again with somebody else. Television is no respecter of persons: it has become, rather, a machine to destroy the person in place of the transient image.

But Richard Dimbleby lasted. I think this was because he was one of those people in whom the public image *was* the private, interior truth. He really believed what he said on *Panorama*. He was unbearably open at moments when lesser men, image-mongers, dissolved into fantasy or fiction. And because he brought only himself to the screen, never a self tarted up to represent the kind of person which viewers or listeners might find desirable, it was because he was himself that you trusted him.

I know he had a lot of qualities which some people found rather plummy, his occasional tendency to cross the boundary from the factual to the magisterial, his incredible unflappability, his open devotion to Queen and Country: but these qualities were aspects of a composite person. They were never caricatures, designed cunningly for effect or viewer appeal. They were part of him. And they were complementary to other qualities which are, perhaps, even less fashionable in modern society – gentleness, patience, respect and charity.

There have been moments in all our lives which have been appreciated and savoured and made history by Dimbleby. I think his great occasion for me will always be his commentary on the funeral of Sir Winston. Here was a figure out of history, an old lonely man going to his long home and taking with him something of the glory of England. You might say that in his death England saw a final end to the dangerous myth of her superior moral authority in a wicked world. Dimbleby did not show it to us like that: he reminded us Churchill was a man, and when, in the closing minutes of that January afternoon, he talked of Bladon and the old men and maidens, young men and children, among whom in English soil Winston would soon be laid to rest, you could hear that Dimbleby himself was openly crying.

He must have known he himself was dying then. In losing him at the end of a year of national bereavement we lost a friend whose wisdom and quietness will linger with us as a reminder that we each have it in us to be a person and that the person, not the image, is holy.

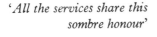

'All the services share this sombre honour'

*By the spring of 1965 the growth of Dimbleby's cancer was accelerating.
He was ill at ease in April when he introduced a television programme com-
memorating some of the great broadcasts made by his American colleague
of nearly thirty years' standing, Edward R. Murrow, who had died of lung
cancer.*

*'Jesus wept' – two words of exasperation from a Dimbleby racked with
pain, which reverberated round the world from the Royal Tour of Germany
in May 1965. To most people, but not to some clergymen, Dimbleby had
made an appalling irreverent blunder. Richard Francis was his Panorama
producer during the Royal Tour of Germany:*

RICHARD FRANCIS

Edward R. Murrow

'Jesus Wept'

It happened at the end of a tough day, Thursday 27 May. For hours
the commentators of a dozen or more television networks had been
doing their separate commentaries from Berlin on the Queen's crowded
progress round the city. Several times there had been technical break-
downs on the links between Berlin and West Germany. And Richard
had to fit his commentary spells in with coverage of the First Test from
Edgbaston.

Now, at 8.50 p.m., we were due to transmit from Berlin to Great
Britain the edited highlights of the day, with a description, live on the
circuit, by Richard. But to our horror all communication with London
was lost just as the programme was about to go on the air. Six minutes
late one vision line and one sound one were reopened and off we went.
Richard was in good form and the delay soon seemed unimportant.
But after two minutes, on another line, back came a message: London
was not receiving us. We checked back, they were getting neither sound
nor vision. Reluctantly we stopped the videotape. 'Richard', I said
aloud, 'hold everything. We're not on the air. London isn't getting us.'

'Jesus wept.'

Which would have passed unnoticed, if London was not in fact receiving us perfectly! After a furious control-line conversation we started
up again, still under the impression London hadn't heard a word. What
we did was to repeat the first couple of minutes. Richard's professionalism made it worse; his introduction was word for word the same!

The supreme irony was yet to come. Despite losing the first ten
minutes we were now ordered to end on schedule, at 9.15. And that meant
fading the recording *just* as the Queen was approaching the Berlin wall.
What an anti-climax.

Richard for once was silent at the end of a programme. More precisely
he was speechless – with anger. Anger not for himself, but because he
hated any BBC programme to fail, particularly one like this. There was
no getting away from it, it had been a shambles. Glumly we thanked
our hosts, ZDF; it was not their fault. The tension was only broken
when one of the German engineers approached Richard and clicked

Berlin Wall, 27 May 1965

his heels. 'Mr Dimbleby I thank you very much. I am tonight very honoured. I always wanted to work with your BBC.'

Of course Richard knew Berlin well. Before and at the end of the war, and later with the building of the Wall, he had made many broadcasts from there. The day before the Queen arrived, as was his wont, he had driven round the route she was going to take. Typically when he got to the Potsdamerplatz he told of his previous broadcasts from the place. There was the time in 1939 when he had described a mass rally passing down the Potsdamerstrasse and through the Platz. In their day they were to Berlin what Regent Street and Piccadilly Circus are to London today. Now they are desolate and deserted, and divided by the Wall. And just on the Western side he found the nail-head in the cobbles driven in at the end of the war to mark the limits of the American, British and Russian sectors. It was from this point that he had introduced *Panorama* on the night of 31 July 1961. Two weeks later the Wall was built.

At the Brandenburger Tor he stopped the car and got out. He saw an opportunity to gather something of the real flavour of life at the Wall. Two British M.P.s were manning an observation box at the bottom of the Street of 17th June. Recognising Richard they welcomed him to their raised platform. Fifteen minutes and a few small but revealing observations later, Richard continued his tour. The next day, when the Queen arrived at the Wall, his commentary was that little bit richer.

Richard spent most of the month of May 1965 either on or in the air. He started by flying the Atlantic three times in four days. After filming 'New York's Finest', the police, he returned to introduce the Early Bird inaugural programme from London. The same night he flew out to introduce *Panorama* from Wall Street. Next day he rushed back to prepare for 'VE+20' with Monty and Ike taking part. That was the programme in which Richard took viewers round Churchill's underground War Room, and proudly introduced David Dimbleby's commentary from Belsen. After that a crowded fortnight following the Queen round Germany and continuing with *Panorama* each Monday.

Walter Cronkite and General of the Army Dwight D. Eisenhower in New York talking to Richard Dimbleby and Field-Marshal Viscount Montgomery in Churchill's War Room in London

Seventeen transmissions and a dozen flights in one month.

It had been a tough ten days since Her Majesty started the tour. The night before she was due to arrive, Richard introduced *Panorama* from the Hotel Petersburg, at Königswinter. Two hours before we went on the air there was a terrible thunderstorm, and rain got into everything. When the programme started, we in the control van could not hear what Richard was saying. Never mind, we thought, he will follow the pictures. We didn't know that his monitor had packed up just before transmission and he was commentating blind – imagining that our pictures were following his words. Fortunately he repeated almost exactly what he said in rehearsal, the pictures matched, and very few viewers would have noticed.

On the first evening of the Queen's trip Richard was asked to comment on the arrival of Her Majesty for the banquet at Schloss Bruehl. This was due at 7.25 London time and so would fit in well with the end of *Tonight*. It would take about ten minutes.

Unfortunately the royal car was delayed nearly half an hour. Richard, as ever, continued implacably although the pictures offered little to talk about. Anxiously London demanded information about the Queen and why she was late. So too did Richard, with anguished facial expressions whilst he talked. The German police were approached; they knew she had left for the banquet but had no idea how far she had got. There were enormous crowds blocking the route. German Television were approached; they knew nothing. Then their producer had an idea: 'Perhaps Herr Dimbleby knows?'

Richard was never the luckiest of people with his flights. Coming back from Hamburg at the end of the Royal Tour his Trident had to make an emergency landing. All three of the hydraulic systems failed in turn, and the plane was left without any brakes. It headed for Amsterdam, the nearest alternative airport, and Richard went back to exchange a jolly word with the rest of the BBC party. To his amazement he saw a block of seats occupied by London policemen in uniform. They had been in Hamburg to embellish the Queen's visit. Jokingly Richard asked them if they were ready to die bravely. According to him, their reaction was to put their helmets on!

Dimbleby had been disappointed at missing a university. He was particularly gratified when the University of Sheffield decided to award him the honorary degree of Doctor of Laws in July 1965.

The Public Orator, Professor Laughton, presented him to the Chancellor, Lord Butler of Saffron Walden, who had frequently met Dimbleby in the Panorama studio, with these unwittingly prescient words:

ERIC LAUGHTON

Honorary LL.D.

If a national opinion poll were to be held, to discover the personality whose disappearance from the television screen would leave the largest gap, the nation's choice might well fall on Richard Dimbleby. In the event of such a calamity, severe as would be the loss (especially on Monday evenings) of that expansive and reassuring presence, it would be still more grievous to lose the voice which for a quarter of a century, at great moments in our history, has expressed the thoughts and feelings of Everyman.

To some of us that voice first became familiar during the War, reporting from battlefields and bringing to the listener at home a new sense of immediacy and involvement. As first BBC war correspondent, Dimbleby served in many areas, and by 1945, when he entered Berlin with British troops, he was marked out as a commentator of singular talent and resourcefulness. Hence, though he left its staff in 1945, the British Broadcasting Corporation has continued to enlist his services, especially in the television presentation of many historic occasions, ranging from the ceremonial pomp of a Coronation or the moving solemnity of a State funeral to the organised chaos of a General Election. To these and other assignments, where faulty timing or a single false note would have been disastrous, Dimbleby has invariably brought skill and imagination in handling his material, an utterance fluent and appropriate, free alike from rhetoric and from bathos, retaining – even off the record – the directness and simplicity of the Authorised Version, and withal an imperturbability which is not disconcerted when Queens are late or Early Birds fail to materialise.

Dimbleby's art is so effectively concealed that it sometimes receives less than its due. Those who criticise him for leaning towards the Establishment are in fact complimenting him on his unfailing ability, at a given moment, to make articulate the feelings of most of his audience. The apparent ease with which he fills out his narrative, whenever necessary, with apt information comes not merely from quickness of mind, but from the careful preparation of a craftsman, born and trained in the newspaper world, who takes a professional pride in thorough workmanship.

A believer in order and tradition, he is no mouthpiece of received opinion, as his own programme *Panorama* makes evident each week. He enjoys the good things of life, including the largest car ever seen outside the portals of Television Centre, with a liveried chauffeur who, it is said, is normally a good deal smarter than his employer.

If our ceremony today be regarded as an acknowledgment of the contribution which television can make to education in the widest sense, let it not escape notice that we have chosen for honour a man to whose good taste and integrity, no less than to his exceptional talents, television in this country owes much of its high repute.

Chancellor, I present to you Richard Dimbleby, as eminently worthy to receive the Degree of Doctor of Laws *honoris causa*.

The University entertained the honorary graduates to lunch before continuing with the Degree Congregation in the afternoon. One who was present recalls:

'Because of the shortness of time, it was not intended that there should be any speeches, but when the toast of the honorary graduates was proposed by the Vice-Chancellor and drunk by the company, which included most of the senior members of staff and their wives, it became clear that a speech must be forthcoming. All eyes turned to Dimbleby, and a rattling of cutlery became louder and more insistent. Eventually he was drawn to his feet by this spontaneous demonstration of friendliness and regard, and spoke briefly and elegantly, and with great sincerity. It was a beautiful piece of impromptu utterance, perfectly adapted to the occasion.'

As Richard stepped into his car to depart Arthur Howick, the liveried chauffeur mentioned in the citation, and a man to whom Richard was devoted, happily addressed him as 'Dr Dimbleby'.

The Pope in New York

Ray Scherer

To Richard's deep disappointment his doctors told him he was too ill to fly to Japan in August with other members of the team for Panorama's 430th edition. Most of the programme came from Nagasaki, just twenty years after the atomic bomb explosion which had ended World War II. Richard had to stay in the studio. He announced the date of Panorama's return after the summer break under its new editor Jeremy Isaacs and added, as some thought modestly, 'I hope to be in attendance'. He was expressing a real and far from certain hope. Meanwhile it had been announced that Pope Paul VI would visit the United Nations on Monday 4 October 1965. The first visit of a Pope to American shores was a great television occasion, both for Eurovision and for Panorama that Monday evening. Richard Dimbleby undertook what turned out to be his last journey abroad, and his last great broadcasting event. Again Richard Francis was the Panorama producer with him:

RICHARD FRANCIS

With the Pope in New York

Richard arrived in the BBC New York office late on Friday 1 October. Although it was after 11 p.m. on his time-scale he immediately set about the task of gathering information. Which were the best books on this and that, who was the best man to talk to about the Catholic hierarchy in the States, how accurately was the Pope's schedule known?

Next day, the Saturday, he attended the briefings held by the UN television unit and CBS. They, with Italian Television, were co-ordinating the programme for all the European networks. Eurovision of course took a common picture sent over the Early Bird satellite. On this occasion the rival American networks also took a common picture. They forsook competition in favour of pooling their resources to get the best coverage of the event. Significantly, at these briefings, the American producers could never quite place Richard among the other commentators. One felt perhaps they would have been happier if he had chaired the meeting. Their solution was to refer all conclusions to him before finalising, 'How d'you reckon that's gonna make out, Dick?'

Richard had not been feeling well since his arrival. 'Something I've eaten' he dismissed it, although he was running a high temperature. Nevertheless, on the Saturday evening he went to two parties. The first was with Peter Woods, former BBC colleague and now ITN's correspondent in New York. He was doing Independent Television's commentary on the Monday. Then on to Eddi Ploman, who was running the United Nations coverage. By now he could not eat a thing, but he was still very much the life and centre of the party.

At 10 o'clock on Sunday morning a large black open car drew up outside the Algonquin Hotel in West 44th Street. It was a sunny, though fresh, autumn morning, but Richard insisted that the hood remain down for the drive round the Pope's route. He wanted to see as much detail as possible.

Ed Stutley, the 20-stone coloured driver, made his living by driving

163

and showing people round Manhattan. Up the long Third Avenue into Harlem he was pointing out the very blocks occupied by Italians, Puerto Ricans, Spanish and Negroes in the polyglot community. Richard made careful notes. But later on, coming back through Central Park, Richard took up the story. 'That's the open-air restaurant where . . .', 'on the next corner is Carnegie Hall . . .', 'there's Tiffany's, where His Holiness is *not* expected for breakfast . . .'. It was an entertainment in itself.

The great day was not without incident. After the 25-mile drive to St Patrick's Cathedral in Fifth Avenue, the Pope retired to Cardinal Spellman's residence to rest before meeting President Johnson. Meanwhile BBC–1 slipped in the transmission of *Blue Peter*. On returning to New York viewers were just in time to see the Pope emerge from the residence. The timing was perfect, it seemed as if he had been cued.

Now Richard began the build-up to the historic moment. 'This will be the first time a Pope has met a President in the United States. . . .' 'All over Europe and particularly in Italy millions of people are watching and waiting for this, one of the highlights of the day. . . .' The Pope entered the lift at the Waldorf Astoria; on the top floor President Johnson was known to be waiting. Imagine the let-down when there appeared on the screen not the President but an American television commentator. Quickly Richard explained, 'that is of course our NBC colleague, Ray Scherer . . .'. Thinking it was a temporary switching error, he flannelled. Not at all. Unknown to us, there had been a last-minute change of plan. The President would see the Pope in private first, the cameras would be let in later. It took some time to establish even that. The Eurovision control room was bedlam. Limply the several European commentators had to round off their commentaries and return viewers to their studios. One of the Italian producers turned to us, 'Richard was able to make it sound like nothing happened, yes?'

Half an hour before he was due to introduce *Panorama* from the UN, Richard was already cooped up in the interpreter's box he was using for his commentary. Scarcely larger than a telephone kiosk, it overlooked not the General Assembly but the Trusteeship Council Chamber. So for the Pope's Address he would have to rely on his monitor. He was checking over his homework when the British party, Lord Caradon, Lord Chalfont and the Foreign Secretary, Michael Stewart, passed by. Lord Caradon stopped, 'Richard, how nice to see you. What are you doing here? Wouldn't you rather come and work in our room nearby?' Richard declined, he wouldn't leave his post at that stage.

By the time the Pope had finished speaking, and we were off the air, it was late evening in London. But to us it was still only afternoon. Richard felt flat. 'What about a really good dinner tonight, Sardi's or somewhere?' we suggested. No, he couldn't face it, he was still off his food. 'What I'd really like to do,' he confessed, 'is to see *Hello Dolly*. It's the one show I've missed.'

Although it had been running on Broadway for nearly two years, 'Dolly' was still sold out for months ahead. At two hours' notice it looked impossible. Sue Goldman of the BBC New York office rang the theatre. 'Any chance of two really good seats for tonight?' 'For tonight!

You're kidding. . . . Anyway, who are they for?' 'Richard Dimbleby.' 'Mr Dimbleby? Well now, Mr Dimbleby we *can* accommodate.' For a couple of hours he really enjoyed himself.

Opposite: U Thant

LEONARD MIALL

Last Days

Leaving New York Richard again had an unlucky flight. His aircraft could not get beyond Shannon. He sat on a bench at the airport until well after dawn, uncomplaining, but unusually quiet. He introduced two more Panoramas. But the New York illness and temperature persisted. It was thought that he had picked up gastro-enteritis in New York, or had reacted to a TAB injection, or perhaps there had been a resurgence of his 1937 paratyphoid. His doctors suspected a gall bladder infection and told him so. Richard said philosophically, 'You'd have thought it enough to have cancer. Now I have to have a gall bladder as well.'

It was announced that he had entered St Thomas's Hospital for observation of suspected gall bladder infection, and this is what both he and his doctors then genuinely believed was keeping him from his Panorama place.

But after an operation it was discovered that a secondary and widespread growth of cancer had given him the symptoms of a gall bladder infection. On 5 November Richard with characteristic courage and

165

common sense told his son David to explain clearly why he was in hospital:

'My father first contracted cancer over five years ago and has been undergoing treatment at various times since then. He asked me to explain this because he is very strongly opposed to the idea of cancer being an unmentionable disease. The reason he has not mentioned it is that in the last five years he has not lost a single day's work because of it, but as he expects to be away for a few weeks he thought that people should know why.'

The news of Richard's illness and the manner of its telling gave his friends, known and unknown, both sadness and enhanced respect. Over 7,000 wrote to him in the hospital. They included many ordinary people who suspected they had cancer and now were given the courage to consult their doctors. His announcement dramatically lifted a taboo. Large numbers of people found they could use a word they had always avoided before. The 'Nursing Mirror' was to write:

'Any public figure has special opportunity for service denied to the man in the street, but does not always recognise it, or use it. In Mr Dimbleby's case, the opportunity was seen, seized with both hands, and utilised to create an impact on this country which will surely never be forgotten, and which promises to be the forerunner of a change in attitude which will affect the lives of millions of people in the future.'

One day a uniformed guardsman arrived bearing champagne from the Queen. Other members of the Royal Family also asked to be kept informed of his progress. Both Lord Fisher of Lambeth and Cardinal Heenan sought to visit him, but few except his immediate family were allowed to his bedside. Dilys Dimbleby never left him.

On Sunday 19 December, Paul Fox went to the hospital:

'He brushed aside all questions about himself. His interests even then centred on the people at Lime Grove; on the programmes; on the audiences. The past he had enshrined did not matter to him. His thoughts, as ever, were on the future.'

The next night, as Panorama ended, James Mossman spoke to camera:

'There are many kinds of courage and it's appropriate for me to refer to a particular example of it tonight. Richard Dimbleby, who has always been here to give an end-of-term flourish to the last *Panorama* of the year, is, as everyone knows, ill in hospital, and as everyone also knows, he was a very sick man long before he took time for hospital treatment, though he never during that time gave any intimation to colleagues, or viewers, of the strain he must have been feeling. That is what is known as professionalism, as well as courage. And what I would like to say, to Richard, because I hope he is watching, is that all of us here in *Panorama*, both on the screen and behind it, send you our very best wishes. I know all of you do also, judging from the seven thousand letters he has received. Yesterday he told a colleague of mine who visited him that he particularly wanted us to pass on his thanks tonight, and to wish all of you a Happy Christmas from him.'

Richard did see, and appreciated, that part of the programme. Two days later, on Wednesday 22 December 1965, he fell into a coma. Shortly after 9 p.m., with Dilys, David and Jonathan at his bedside, he died. He was 52.

166

BBC-2 made a special announcement of the news of his death at 9.30 p.m. BBC-1 waited until the end of the play at 10 p.m. ITV paid an unprecedented tribute to a respected competitor by interrupting programmes for two minutes. The entire '24 Hours' programme at 10.15 p.m. became a television obituary in which many tributes were paid, including this from the Controller of Television Programmes, Huw Wheldon:

HUW WHELDON

What can we do except mourn him?

Richard Dimbleby was irreplaceable as far as we are concerned here. It is not simply that he was the supreme professional that people saw. The reason producers liked to have him handling their programmes was that you knew that the preparation would be absolutely meticulous, you knew that in the event he would be totally imperturbable and, no matter what had happened, the situation would be good-humoured and you would be looking forward to tomorrow and other days. But I have always felt that the word "professional" was used too easily about him, because he was something bigger than simply a very, very professional man. He had a quality which I can only call dignity. He died with dignity, as he lived and worked with dignity.

And over and above both professionalism and dignity, he had the gift, which is very rare, not simply of brilliantly finding the apt phrase and the graceful sentence, but, when called upon to do it, of being able to speak on your behalf and mine. He was the voice of the BBC on thousands of occasions, and on hundreds occasions I think he was even the voice of the nation. To an extent I think incomparable in the history of radio or television so far as this country is concerned, he was the voice of our generation, and probably the most telling voice on BBC radio or television of any kind in this country so far. It is in that sense I feel he is irreplaceable, and what can we do except mourn him?

Half the Independent Television Programme Companies rebroadcast the BBC's Tribute programme in its entirety. The other half broadcast a special tribute mounted by Granada Television. Later Michael Peacock, Richard's first producer of Panorama and the General Election programmes, spoke in the BBC Television News:

MICHAEL PEACOCK

The Hallmark of Quality

At a moment like this when so many things could be said about Richard Dimbleby I only want to say three things. The first is that he really was the greatest professional broadcasting has ever known. No other man gave so much that was unique to both radio and television. He set standards of performance and conduct which will never be excelled. He truly was a master of his craft, head and shoulders above everyone else in skill, integrity and dedication. For broadcasting and especially for television his loss is a tragic one, there never will be another like him, and television will never be quite the same now that he's gone.

Secondly I must underline the extraordinary courage that he showed during the past five and a half years. To this day, I don't know how he managed to keep going, never missing a programme, always managing to summon up from some deep, apparently limitless reserve of will-power and courage the extra energy and stamina that he needed – not just for his job but to put upon his programmes the hallmark of quality. And to all of us who know what he must have endured during the election results marathon, Telstar spectaculars, royal weddings and so on, his is a quite incredible story of courage which will, I'm sure, be recalled with wonder and admiration for many, many years to come.

And lastly, it should be said that Richard was really a wonderful person to have known. Behind the dignity of his public image, with the almost automatic association of his name with *Panorama* and the coverage of great occasions, behind the face known to millions, was a warm and delightful man, intelligent, full of fun, kind-hearted, patient, courteous, above all devoted to his family, to his four children and to Dilys his wife who shared so bravely his long and private fight for life. For them, this is of course a time of intense and private grief, and for all of us who were lucky enough to have known him as a friend and colleague this is a moment of deep and lasting sorrow and a sad, sad ending to the year.

The next morning the BBC carried this radio tribute in Today:

JAMES MOSSMAN

The Most Disciplined Performer

When I first joined *Panorama* seven years ago, I remember Richard Dimbleby telling me on location in some flooded British town that it was all very well to have a good degree and be bright, but what was really needed in television was discipline. And he was, in fact, the most disciplined performer I've ever seen. He approached his job like an artist or an engineer, and to watch him linking a show or doing a commentary on a big public event was to see technical perfection. He loved his work, not only television but all work. He loved being busy and he loved the challenge of complicated situations in which he'd be obliged to follow one set of events from a monitor screen, for example, with one eye whilst keeping pace with another set of events with the other. He was the only man in British television who became well known in America, because of his work on Telstar and Early Bird, and whenever I've been in New York with him, New Yorkers and especially policemen (for whom he seemed to have a predilection) would salute him at crossroads and say 'Hullo, Richard!'.

I've often talked to other people in the BBC about what the qualities were in Dimbleby that created such an impact on viewers, mostly favourable but not always. And I think the secret was that he reflected many of the key qualities of the English. He was simple, and had a very straightforward and concrete approach to things and situations. He had a strong sentiment and a strong loyalty and I'd say probably did more than anyone else to show the place of the Royal Family in the Sixties. But since the last years of his life were overshadowed by cancer, what I recall most clearly about him was his courage under the strain of it all. I remember coming back with him from a filming outing in New York one afternoon late in autumn. We were much later than we'd expected, and Dimbleby was tired and in quite evident pain, but never during the preceding, extremely tiresome hours had he been impatient or tried to cry off the story. This is professionalism of a very high order and it's this which will be remembered.

Messages of condolence flowed into the BBC from all over the world, especially from the Commonwealth and from countries with particular debts of gratitude to Dimbleby: Yugoslavia, Persia and Greece. The Canadian Broadcasting Corporation broadcast special tributes.

The European Broadcasting Union said: 'His death brings a sense of personal loss as much to us in Europe and beyond as it does to you who live in England.'

North German Radio said: 'He stood for all the qualities which have made BBC Television an example of fearless yet thoroughly honest journalistic work.'

From Moscow Boris Belitzky telegraphed: 'A great voice has gone off the air.'

Fred Friendly cabled from CBS News in New York: 'Richard Dimbleby – BBC – was a dateline all in his own right like Coventry, Parliament, Trafalgar and Dunkirk. His voice, the voice of Britain, and that of Ed Murrow CBS were stilled the same year. These men often meant as much to citizens in each other's countries as they did in their own. We at CBS News are additionally saddened by the death of another friend and colleague whose voice and whose truth all of us can so ill afford to lose.'

But perhaps the message that said most came in halting English from an Italian worker living in Germany:
As foreigner friend and fans's programs of B.B.C. specially in 'PANORAMA' I am really shocked about Mr Dimbley's death, former broadcast man and director of 'PANORAMA'. His face was so familiar and friendly speaking that I really enjoyed so many times watching your program on PANORAMA, so beautifully runned by him. In the same time this hour of sorrow for everybody's feeling will you so kind to have my personal feeling of regret for all family's B.B.C. for such big loss. I am very sorry if I am ask you for a favour and to send my feelings as unknown friend, to Mr Dimbley's wife and my warm cuddle for his sons DAVID and JONATHAN in this hour of big sorrow for them.

Thank you very much for all.

Yours faithfully

FILIPPO PALMERINI

The Dimbleby family received several thousand letters. Many wished to give practical expression to their affection and admiration for Richard. The Richard Dimbleby Cancer Fund was quickly established, to which the profits of this book and of the companion long-playing record will go. The public response was immediate and strong.

Richard Dimbleby sometimes called Westminster Abbey his 'workshop'. On the morrow of his death the Dean of Westminster straightway suggested that a Memorial Service should be held in the great cathedral church where England honours those who have done outstanding service. Moreover the Dean and Chapter decided that none of the substantial expense of holding an Abbey Memorial Service should fall upon either the Dimbleby family or the BBC.

The service on 4 January 1966 was a fitting farewell to the man who had so often been the spokesman of the BBC, and of the nation, at Westminster Abbey's great occasions. The Abbey was freshly adorned and floodlit in celebration of its 900 years. Close to the High Altar a Christmas Tree still stood, with golden bows and bells the only decoration to its dark green branches. Television lighting enhanced the brilliant colouring of the choir stalls and the vestments. For hours beforehand patient queues had formed behind unopened doors.

After every seat was taken, hundreds crowded into the cloister to watch the Memorial Service on television. Others outside the West Door listened to the Sound broadcast on loudspeakers. Five million viewers at home saw the service at 4 p.m., and another six and a half million watched a recording at the end of the evening. Dr Eric Abbott, the Dean of Westminster, conducted the service and read a prayer for broadcasters. The address was given by Dr George Reindorp, Bishop of Guildford:

BISHOP OF GUILDFORD

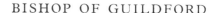

His Example Shone Bright

'Praise my soul the King of Heaven, to His feet thy tribute bring.' And the tribute we now bring is the life, work, art, friendship and love of Richard Dimbleby.

The very mention of his name conjures up in the minds of millions a *person*, someone they felt they knew. Many here in the Abbey did know him personally – those who shaped and shared with him the priceless treasure of a happy home – to whom today our hearts go out in loving sympathy. You in the BBC were his colleagues. So were you in his newspaper for which he cared so much. You all pay tribute here to a man, a friend, a colleague whose work inspired your admiration, marred by never a hint of jealousy.

The measure of his contribution to our English way of life is the fact that almost everyone in England would wish, if they were able at this moment, to give their own picture of what Richard Dimbleby meant to them.

Why is this? Was it because he was a prodigious worker, covering an immense amount of ground in an all too short life? Not entirely, though

Opposite: the broadcast Memorial Service, with Dean of Westminster, mourners in the Abbey, Bishop of Guildford, and Archbishop Lord Fisher

he was certainly that. Was it because he was a superb professional, demanding the highest standards from himself and inspiring all around him to attain them also? Not entirely, though he was a master at his art. Was it because, although broadcasting cannot speak to the individual, broadcasters of genius can nearly seem to do so? Not entirely, though he was certainly one such.

It was because there was something in him which responded to people as people. Queens and cameramen, bishops and bakers, politicians and printers, homes and husbands, craftsmen and children – these were of the stuff of England's green and pleasant land which Richard loved. To describe them to others, to hear their point of view, to admire their craft, to listen to their hopes and fears, to help their fellows to assess their value in the moving line between past and present which we call history – this for Richard made sense to his integrity of soul which was his supreme possession.

And it was just because he knew these people, because something in him responded to the majesty and meaning of what was happening that, in the words of Garter King of Arms, he 'originated and established the new profession and art of commentator on the great occasions and ceremonies of state'. For though he walked with kings and queens, he did not lose the common touch; and knew how by word and by silence to interpret to us ordinary English people throughout the land the outward expression of our heritage and history.

But his unique contribution to our state occasions must not cloud our gratitude for much, much more. A brilliant war reporter, sharing the experiences of fear and danger, his visit to Belsen, one of the first people to go there after the war, left an indelible mark on him. From then on he was never without the knowledge of what can happen to an individual in horrible cruelty, or in squalor; what can happen to those who are unloved or uncared for. And just because of this, the English scene, the English people, their moments grave and gay, gave to him a security which he in turn gave back to them in admiration and service. Richard really cared.

When in those marathon broadcasts about the General Elections Richard Dimbleby announced the results from here or there and added some homely comment about this place or that, you always felt that he was recalling this individual or that whom he had met there. Perhaps it was you in the Abbey, or you in the crowd overflowing the Abbey in the cloister outside, or you viewing, or you listening, or you, or me. And it usually was. For remember that long before *Panorama* became part of the English scene, for five and a half years, for two days a week, Richard was *Down Your Way* touring these islands among the people whom he loved, mindful, as Milton taught him, that 'where there is much desire to learn, there of necessity will be much arguing, many opinions: for opinion in good men is but knowledge in the making'.

And it was to avoid embarrassment to these English people he knew so well that without any fuss or heroics he allowed the secret of his cancer, shared by his family and friends for five years, to be made known to the public who would miss his part in their daily life. And by his action he gave courage and hope to many in the knowledge that if he could face this scourge squarely, so could they. And his example shone bright in a dark day.

Who shall pay the last tribute? Shall it be a Surrey housewife who said: 'He made many things real to me. In an age of shams he was a man of integrity', or shall it be the anonymous writer of perhaps one of the most human of the thousands of letters that poured in to him in hospital:

> Dear Mr Dimbleby,
>
> My wife and children asked me to write to you and say how sorry we are that you are ill, and how much we miss you on *Panorama*.
>
> Who am I? Just an ordinary roadman from Berkshire.
>
> See you down my road one of these days.
>
> Yours faithfully,
The Roadman.

Now Richard has left us. Sometimes as we stand on the shore waving goodbye to a ship – as she fades hull-down on the horizon, lost to our sight, we say 'There she goes', and turn away heavy-hearted. But we forget that there on the further shore eager eyes are watching for her and eager hands stretch out in greeting.

So, too, with Richard. With quiet confidence and deep gratitude and love, we commend him to the King of Heaven, firm in the knowledge that death cannot kill the bond of love which lifts us all above time and space into the heart of God Himself.

Archbishop Lord Fisher spoke the Commendation of the Departed. It referred to Richard Dimbleby's gifts of mind and heart and spirit which 'he improved by care and diligence so great that he established a new art and a new profession of communicating to the people by a commentary the outward forms and the inward meaning of great occasions both in Church and State'.

After the final hymn the fabric of the Abbey rang as the BBC Symphony Orchestra, conducted by Sir Adrian Boult, played 'Nimrod' from Elgar's 'Enigma Variations'. It fell to Wynford Vaughan-Thomas, fellow war correspondent and lifelong friend, to give the closing commentary to the last Richard Dimbleby broadcast:

WYNFORD VAUGHAN-THOMAS

Farewell

The service in the Abbey has been the public commemoration of Richard Dimbleby. May we who worked so long with him, the cameras and microphones now backstage, now say our farewell to the man we knew as the finest professional of us all. Ours is a transient art; our words and pictures make a powerful immediate impact, and then fade as if they had never been. But Richard brought a sense of permanence to our impermanent profession. We knew him as a simple man, a good man, and in the end a very brave man. He gave warmth to the spoken word, friendliness to the formal occasion, and tradition and dignity to the whole new world of broadcasting. We shall not easily forget him.

*Memorial Service:
the empty commentary box,
Sir Adrian Boult, the
family*